U0668327

三级人力资源
管理师（上海）
过关必备

王伟杰 李秀英 ◎ 编

一书在手，考试通过无忧！
汇人商学院独家研发，权威解读，经典诠释，精准定位，事半功倍！

倾力打造 1000 多道理论与案例题库，上海独创，针对上海考试

上海人力资源管理师培训金牌机构，
已培训学员超过3万名，全程通过率达到85%

经济管理出版社
ECONOMY & MANAGEMENT PUBLISHING HOUSE

图书在版编目（CIP）数据

三级人力资源管理师（上海）过关必备/王伟杰，李秀英编 . —北京：经济管理出版社，2017.6（2019.9重印）

ISBN 978 - 7 - 5096 - 5120 - 9

Ⅰ.①三…　Ⅱ.①王…　②李…　Ⅲ.①企业管理—人力资源管理—资格考试—自学参考资料　Ⅳ.①F272.92

中国版本图书馆 CIP 数据核字（2017）第 101563 号

组稿编辑：曹　靖
责任编辑：杨国强　张瑞军
责任印制：黄章平
责任校对：超　凡　王纪慧

出版发行：经济管理出版社
　　　　　（北京市海淀区北蜂窝 8 号中雅大厦 A 座 11 层　　100038）
网　　　址：www. E - mp. com. cn
电　　　话：(010) 51915602
印　　　刷：三河市延风印装有限公司
经　　　销：新华书店
开　　　本：720mm×1000mm/16
印　　　张：20.25
字　　　数：278 千字
版　　　次：2017 年 6 月第 1 版　　2019 年 9 月第 3 次印刷
书　　　号：ISBN 978 - 7 - 5096 - 5120 - 9
定　　　价：59.00 元

编写说明

　　本书是帮助 HR 从业人员学习和参加上海三级人力资源管理师职业资格考试的专用书籍。上海地区的人力资源管理师从 2003 年开考至今，每年参加人数都超过 2 万人，成为国内人力资源管理师职业资格考试参加人数最多的地区。随着 2014 年第二版教材的出版，考试进一步规范化，考试难度不断提高。因此，要想顺利通过考试，必须有丰富翔实和具有针对性的资料，并加上学员本人认真地复习才可以实现一次性通过。

　　本书的编写者都来自上海地区人力资源管理师专业培训机构——汇人网。汇人网从 2003 年开始在上海率先开始从事人力资源管理师培训，现在已经成为上海规模最大、知名度最高的人力资源管理培训机构。本书的主编王伟杰博士作为汇人网的创始人，长期研究企业人力资源管理、劳动关系管理与劳动合同法应用等，出版了多本人力资源与劳动关系、劳动合同法领域的理论研究与实践应用的专业著作。

　　本书为了保证学习效果，书内的理论知识与实务技能、专业英语等习题都没有直接公布答案，建议读者先自学每章知识要点，并独立完成相关题目，全部完成后再行查阅答案，答案公布在汇人网学员论坛 bbs. hr163. com。如有疑问需要咨询，可以加官方 QQ：800008163，微信公众号：汇人，或者致电 4008－363－163 咨询。

汇人网人力资源职业资格考试命题研究组

2017 年 6 月

目 录
Contents

理论知识部分

实务技能单元测试题

专业英语模拟试题

理论知识部分

第一篇
人力资源规划

本篇重点内容：

1. 人力资源需求与供给预测方法和流程

2. 人力资源管理制度建设原则和步骤

3. 人力资源供小于求或供大于求的基本方法

4. 工作分析流程

5. 工作说明书编制

人力资源规划流程：

1. 人力资源战略环境分析

2. 企业人力资源现状评价

3. 人力资源需求预测

4. 人力资源供给预测

5. 协调人力资源供需平衡

6. 人力资源规划实施的监控

一、判断题（下列判断正确的请打"√"，错误的打"×"）

1. 人力资源规划最显著的特点是把员工看成资源。

（　　）

2. 人力资源规划的实质是促进企业实现其目标，它必须具有战略性、前瞻性和目标性的特点。

（　　）

3. 对人力资源信息的审核又称复查，一般采用普查的方式进行。

（　　）

4. 人力资源信息的审核中，如果计算错误导致数据的偏差，要采取修正的方法，通过对原始数据的再次计算进行修改。

（　　）

5. 经验预测法是一种最简单的人力资源需求预测方法。

（　　）

6. 了解企业人力资源数量是为了探求现有人力资源数量是否与企业的业务量相匹配。

（　　）

7. 员工素质分析就是分析现有工作人员的性格特征和心理素质。

（　　）

8. 人力资源需求预测包括现实人力资源需求预测、未来人力资源需求预测和未来流失人力资源需求预测三部分。

（　　）

9. 在人力资源需求预测时，还要掌握预测中的定性、定量、时间和数量四个基本要素。

（　　）

10. 趋势外推法的缺点是过于简单，只能预测人力资源需求的大概趋势，不能提供相关质量数据。

（　　）

11. 人力资源规划包括战略规划、组织规划、人员规划、制度规划和费用规划。

（　　）

12. 人力资源信息分析资料是对企业相关人力资源信息分析的结果，一般以分析报告的形式呈现，称为人力资源信息分析报告。

（　　）

13. 人力资源信息分析报告是人力资源规划的重要依据。

（　　）

14. 社会生产规模大小影响企业人力资源供给。

（　　）

15. 德尔菲法是把专家聚拢在一起集体讨论，做出预测。

（　　）

16. 对于管理人员供给的预测，最简单有效的方法是制订管理人员接替计划。

（　　）

17. 德尔菲法的专家可以是组织内部专家，也可以是外聘专家。

（　　）

18. 马尔可夫分析法，是一种特别的专家意见咨询方法。

（　　）

19. 人力资源信息分析的方法可以分为定性方法和定量方法。

（　　）

20. 马尔可夫分析法适用于企业政策不稳定或有较大变化的企业。

（　　）

21. 合理规划，及时执行，可以达成企业人力资源供求平衡。

（　　）

22. "见人又见物"是以工作任务为中心的管理哲学。

（　　）

23. 以任务为中心的管理哲学把员工视为社会人。

（　　）

24. 以人为中心的管理哲学采取的管理方式是民主—尊敬—参与。

（　　）

25. 以任务为中心的管理哲学着眼于企业的长期目标。

（　　）

26. 国家法律法规明确规定"不应该做什么或不应该怎么做时"，企业千万不能去做；而没有说明"不应该做什么或不应该怎么做时"，企业应该谨慎去做。

（　　）

27. "见物不见人"的管理哲学认为员工是具有能动性的重要资源。

（　　）

28. 企业人力资源管理体系是企业精神、经营理念、价值观念等意识形态的集中表现。

（　　）

29. 一项具体的人力资源管理制度一般应由总则、主文和附则等章节组成。

（　　）

30. 工作分析是把工作的内容、工作的资格条件和报酬结合起来，目的是满足组织的需要。

（　　）

31. 岗位是组织中工作内容自成体系、职责独立的最小业务单元。

（　　）

32. 不相容职务分离的核心是内部牵制。

（　　）

33. 工作设计的主要内容包括工作内容、工作职责和工作关系三个方面。

（　　）

34. 保证工作完整性能增加员工的工作责任感，认识到自己的重要性。

（　　）

35. 组织中的工作关系，表现为协作关系、监督关系等方面。

（　　）

36. 在企业组织整体规划下实现岗位明确分工，在分工基础上又能有效综合，使各岗位职责明确的同时又能同步协调，是工作设计的整分合原则。

（　　）

37. 基于任务的岗位设置是将明确的工作目标按照工作流程的特点层层分解到岗位。

（　　）

38. 工作设计中的组织分析法通常适用于大型企业的重组项目。

（　　）

39. 工作设计中的标杆对照法适用于不太精确的项目。

（　　）

40. 工作设计中的流程优化法适用于较小的项目，主要应用在实施一个新的管理信息系统时。

（　　）

41. 工作设计为组织人力资源管理提供了依据，保证事得其人，人尽其才，人事相宜。

（　　）

42. 工作内容的设计是岗位设计的重点，一般包括工作广度、深度，工作的自主性、完整性，以及工作的反馈性五个方面。

（　　）

43. 基于任务的岗位设置在机器化大工业时代十分突出，其最大的缺点是只考虑任务要求忽视在岗者个人特点。

（　　）

44. 基于团队的岗位设置要求赋予直接管理者更大的责任。

（　　）

45. 基于能力的岗位设置企业内部的岗位管理常常采用的是"宽带"管理。

（　　）

46. 基于团队的岗位设置应用范围不广，更多的是应用在"项目型"公司。

（　　）

47. 工作分析是指收集所有与职位相关的信息，以科学和系统的方法确定某职务的性质、职责、任务和要求，决定一项工作所应包含的内容和从事该工作必备的知识、技术和能力，并提供与职务本身要求相关的其他信息。

（　　）

48. 工作说明书是对工作分析的结果加以整合以形成具有企业法规效力的正式文本。

（　　）

49. 工作分析是人力资源部一个部门的事。

（　　）

50. 工作描述又称岗位标准、任职资格，指任职者要胜任该项工作所必须具备的资格与条件。

（　　）

51. 工作规范是工作说明书的重要组成部分，是对任职者在知识、技能等方面的最低要求，关注的是完成工作任务所需的人的特质。

（　　）

52. 通过对员工类别进行分析，可以体现一个企业的业务重心所在。

（　　）

53. 工作说明书要准确地说明某项工作的具体要求和任职资格条件。这是工作说明书的完备性。

（　　）

54. 一份完整的工作说明书包括工作描述和工作规范两大方面的内容。

（　　）

55. 协调费用最小原则是为减少不同职位间的协调，降低运作成本。

（　　）

56. 技能清单法尤其是在公司裁员或者改变组织结构时尤为重要。

（　　）

57. 人力资源管理制度体现了物质存在与精神意识的统一。

（　　）

58. 企业员工的理想年龄分配应当呈金字塔形。

（　　）

59. 人力资源信息处理的定性方法通常包括统计分组法和综合法。

（　　）

60. 在现实中，企业不仅应该编写好工作说明书，更要用好工作说明书，以优化人力资源管理系统，提高人力资源管理水平。

（　　）

二、单项选择题（下列每题的选项中，只有 1 个是正确的）

1. （　　） 不属于常用的人力资源信息。

A. 人力资源数量

B. 员工类别

C. 职位结构

D. 岗位职责

2. （　　） 体现一个企业的业务重心所在。

A. 员工类别

B. 员工素质

C. 年龄结构

D. 职位结构

3. （　　） 不属于人力资源信息审核的内容。

A. 及时性

B. 完整性

C. 实用性

D. 准确性

4. 人力资源信息的审核又称审查，一般采用（　　） 的方式进行。

A. 分析

B. 统计

C. 抽样

D. 普查

5. （　　） 不是人力资源需求预测时要掌握的基本要素。

A. 定性要素

B. 定量要素

C. 时间要素

D. 方法要素

6. （ ）的目标是通过专家们各自的意见来预测某一领域的发展，是一种特别的专家意见咨询方法。

A. 现状规划法

B. 马尔可夫法

C. 技能清单法

D. 德尔菲法

7. （ ）属于人力资源需求预测的方法。

A. 德尔菲法

B. 马尔可夫法

C. 技能清单法

D. 劳动力市场分析

8. （ ）不是影响人力资源需求的外部因素。

A. 劳动力市场变化

B. 政府相关政策变化

C. 企业目标的变化

D. 行业发展状况变化

9. （ ）是找出人事变动的规律，以此推测未来人事变动趋势的一种常用方法。

A. 德尔菲法

B. 马尔可夫法

C. 技能清单法

D. 标杆法

10. 人力资源信息审核的（　　）是指要检查信息内容是否合理、统计口径是否一致、计算是否准确、计量单位是否合适、前后是否一致等。

A. 及时性

B. 完整性

C. 准确性

D. 实用性

11. （　　）是人力资源需求预测中最复杂也是最精确的一种方法。

A. 多元学习回归预测法

B. 一元线性回归预测法

C. 计算机模拟预测法

D. 趋势外推法

12. 使用（　　）进行人力资源需求预测时，必须避免专家们面对面地集体讨论。

A. 标杆法

B. 马尔可夫法

C. 趋势外推法

D. 德尔菲法

13. 相对而言，下面几种人力资源需求预测方法中，（　　）最为简单。

A. 工作负荷预测法

B. 现状规划法

C. 德尔菲法

D. 经验预测法

14. 下列（　　）不是人力资源供给预测的方法。

A. 现状规划法

B. 马尔可夫法

C. 技能清单法

D. 管理人员接替计划法

15. 企业要求下属各部门、单位根据各自的生产任务、技术设备等变化的情况，对本单位将来对各种人员的需求进行综合预测，然后把下属各部门的预测数据进行综合平衡，从中预测出整个组织将来某一时期内对各种人员的需求总数，是（　　）。

A. 工作负荷预测法

B. 现状规划法

C. 德尔菲法

D. 分合性预测法

16. 如果一个组织中主管职位太多，可能导致组织结构不合理，管理控制幅度（　　）。

A. 太大

B. 太狭窄

C. 不变

D. 不确定

17. 技能档案是预测（　　）的有效工具。

A. 人力资源需求

B. 人力资源平衡

C. 人力资源供给

D. 人力资源流失

18. （　　）不是影响人力资源供求平衡的影响因素。

A. 人员流动

B. 培训与开发

C. 绩效管理

D. 工作分析

19. 当企业人力资源供不应求时，不应采取（   ）。

A. 将符合条件且富余的人调往空缺职位

B. 聘用临时工

C. 提高企业资本技术构成，提高生产率

D. 全员轮训

20. 在建立人力资源制度体系时，首先要解决好核心的问题，即（   ）。

A. 企业文化的建设和企业精神的培育等问题

B. 员工生产效率问题

C. 管理技能问题

D. 企业沟通问题

21. （   ）不是人力资源管理制度建设的原则。

A. 促进企业与员工共同发展原则

B. 严格遵守国家法律法规原则

C. 客观公正原则

D. 根据企业的变化情况不断调整的原则

22. （   ）是一种特别的专家意见咨询方法，是一种能避免专家之间的相互影响及"从众行为"，并能够逐步达成一致意见的结构化方法。

A. 德尔菲法

B. 马尔可夫法

C. 技能清单法

D. 标杆法

23. （   ）的参与能够提高工作分析的有效性和接受性。

A. 高层管理者

B. 直线经理

C. 人力资源部

D. 任职者

24. 企业人力资源管理制度体系可以分为基础性管理制度和（　　）两个方面。

A. 综合性管理制度

B. 员工管理制度

C. 核心管理制度

D. 生产经营管理制度

25. 下面不属于人力资源管理保持职能的主要活动的是（　　）。

A. 促使员工充分发挥潜质

B. 有效激励员工

C. 提供安全健康的工作环境和条件，营造良好的企业文化氛围

D. 通过奖惩、解聘、晋升等方法，确保员工技能水平和工作效率达到岗位要求

26. （　　）不属于员工管理制度。

A. 工作时间规定

B. 员工奖惩规定

C. 女工计划生育规定

D. 员工培训与开发规定

27. 企业内部的岗位管理常常采用"宽带"管理的是（　　）。

A. 基于能力的岗位设置

B. 基于任务的岗位设置

C. 基于团队的岗位设置

D. 基于项目的岗位设置

28. 在工作设计时，（　　）适用于大型企业的大范围重组项目。

A. 组织分析法

B. 关键使命法

C. 流程优化法

D. 标杆对照法

29. 在工作设计时，（　　）适用于较小项目，主要运用在一个新的管理信息系统。

A. 组织分析法

B. 关键使命法

C. 流程优化法

D. 标杆对照法

30. 工作说明书包括工作描述和（　　）两部分。

A. 工作能力

B. 工作内容

C. 工作规范

D. 工作职责

31. 对于工作量不足80%的岗位，及时进行撤岗、并岗，保证每一个岗位的负荷，使所有工作尽可能集中，以降低人工成本，是工作分析中（　　）的要求。

A. 专业分工原则

B. 协调费用最小原则

C. 不相容职务分离原则

D. 整分合原则

32. 奖惩、解聘等属于（　　）职能。

A. 录用

B. 保持

C. 发展

D. 调整

33.（　　）界定工作人员在工作活动内容上的权限范围、层级与控制力度。

A. 工作描述

B. 工作权限

C. 工作内容

D. 工作对象

34.（　　）是指对与工作相关的工具、技术和方法的运用。

A. 工作技能要求

B. 工作能力

C. 解决问题能力

D. 协调能力

35. 工作说明书中每项内容应是被分析的各种工作共有的，不同工作之间可以相互参照比较，有利于确定工作的相对价值，为薪酬体系建立和考核提供参考依据。这体现工作说明书的（　　）。

A. 系统性

B. 实用性

C. 普遍性

D. 简约性

36. 认识到自己工作的重要性，使员工工作的责任心增强，工作的热情提高是（　　）要实现的目的。

A. 工作的广度

B. 工作的深度

C. 工作的自主性

D. 工作的反馈性

37. 在整体规划下实现岗位明确分工，在分工基础上又能有效地综合，使各岗位职责明确的同时又能同步协调，是工作设计的（　　）。

A. 专业分工原则

B. 协调费用最小原则

C. 不相容职务分离原则

D. 整分合原则

38. 从整个组织愿景和使命出发，设计基本组织模型。然后依据具体业务流程需要，设计不同的岗位，属于工作设计方法的（　　）。

A. 组织分析法

B. 关键使命法

C. 流程优化法

D. 标杆对照法

39. 假定企业保持原有的生产和技术不变，则企业的人力资源也应处于相对稳定状态，即企业各种人员的配备比例和人员的总数将完全能适应预测规划期内人力资源的需要，这种方法是（　　）。

A. 工作负荷预测法

B. 德尔菲法

C. 现状规划法

D. 分合性预测法

40. 人力资源需求预测分为现实人力资源需求预测、未来人力资源需求预测和（　　）三部分。

A. 现实人力资源供给

B. 未来流失人力资源需求预测

C. 现实人力资源流失

D. 未来人力资源预算需求

41. （　　）是适用于不太精确的项目范围的工作设计方法。

A. 组织分析法

B. 关键使命法

C. 流程优化法

D. 标杆对照法

42. （　　）不是工作分析小组成员。

A. 企业高层管理者

B. 工作分析人员

C. 外部专家

D. 职工代表

43. 制订工作分析计划、审核和检查工作流程，是（　　）的职责。

A. 人力资源部

B. 直线经理

C. 公司高层领导

D. 外部专家和顾问

44. 以（　　）为目标的工作说明书可以不包括任职资格。

A. 招聘甄选

B. 培训开发

C. 绩效考核

D. 薪酬管理

45. （　　）不是任职者在工作分析中的职责。

A. 参加数据收集

B. 参与工作分析面谈

C. 参与工作说明书草案的制订

D. 参与工作分析的制订

46. （　　）是预测人力资源供给的有效工具。

A. 技能档案

B. 人力资源需求曲线

C. 管理人员接替计划

D. 领导定额预测

47. （　　）是人力资源需求预测中最复杂也是最精确的一种方法。

A. 多元学习回归预测法

B. 一元线性回归预测法

C. 计算机模拟预测法

D. 趋势外推法

48. 保证（　　）能使员工有成就感。

A. 工作的深度

B. 工作的完整性

C. 工作的自主性

D. 工作的反馈性

49. 行为确定等级评价法大多数使用（　　）这个术语，表示构成工作的任务和责任的广泛范畴。

A. 工作维度

B. 工作力度

C. 工作强度

D. 工作态度

50. 李某总是认为人的本性是积极的，并能主动地完成工作，承担责任。李某的管理方法在对人的定位上认为人是（　　）。

A."机器人"

B."经济人"

C."生活人"

D."社会人"

51. 基于（　　）的岗位设置是一种比较理想的岗位设置。

A. 能力

B. 团队

C. 任务

D. 项目

52. 从整个组织的远景和使命出发，设计一个基本的组织模型，然后根据具体的业务流程需要，设计不同的岗位，属于工作设计方法的（　　）。

A. 组织分析法

B. 关键使命法

C. 流程优化法

D. 标杆对照法

53. 工作说明书既要反映现实又要预见未来。这体现了工作说明书的（　　）。

A. 预见性

B. 实用性

C. 普遍性

D. 简约性

54.（　　）不是人力资源部门在工作分析中的职责。

A. 制订工作分析计划

B. 对直线经理和任职者进行培训

C. 提供工作分析专业知识

D. 为执行工作分析的多方面工作授权

55. （　　）是以任务为中心的管理哲学的管理方式。

A. 民主—尊敬—参与

B. 权利—命令—服从

C. 沟通—协调—合作

D. 着眼于企业长远发展

56. 基于（　　）的岗位设置在第三产业占主导的时代很显著。

A. 能力

B. 任务

C. 团队

D. 项目

57. 工作描述的核心内容包括工作标识、工作概要、工作关系和(　　)。

A. 工作权限

B. 工作负荷

C. 工作职责

D. 工作环境与工作条件

58. 企业经营活动中的授权、签发、核准、执行和记录等工作步骤必须有相对独立的人员或部门分别实施或执行，是工作分析中（　　）的要求。

A. 专业分工原则

B. 协调费用最小原则

C. 不相容职务分离原则

D. 整分合原则

59. （　　）不是影响人力资源需求的内部因素。

A. 企业目标变化

B. 行业发展状况变化

C. 组织形式变化

D. 企业最高领导层的理念

60.（　　）是导致员工损耗的因素。

A."拉力"和"推力"

B."拉力"

C."推力"

D. 吸引力

三、多项选择题（下列每题的选项中，至少有 2 个是正确的）

1. 人力资源规划主要由制度规划、人员规划、（　　）等构成。

A. 战略规划

B. 费用规划

C. 职业规划

D. 组织规划

2.（　　）是影响企业人力资源供求平衡的因素。

A. 业务高速发展

B. 人员流动

C. 培训与开发

D. 绩效管理

E. 工作设计

3. 分析组织的员工年龄结构，可以得出公司的平均年龄，员工年轻化还是日趋老化，以及（　　）等。

A. 员工吸收新知识、新技术的能力

B. 员工工作的体能负荷

C. 员工离职率和流动率预测

D. 工作职位和职务的性质与年龄大小的可能的匹配要求

4. 人力资源信息非常丰富，常用的人力资源信息有（　　）。

A. 人力资源数量

B. 员工类别

C. 员工素质

D. 年龄结构

5. 下面企业人力资源供大于求的时候会采用的常用方法是（　　）。

A. 加强培训工作

B. 减少员工工作时间

C. 制订全员轮训计划

D. 合并和关闭机构

6. 人力资源管理制度建设的原则包括（　　）。

A. 促进企业与员工共同发展原则

B. 紧密结合企业实际情况原则

C. 严格遵守国家法律法规原则

D. 根据企业的变化情况不断进行调整的原则

7. 工作内容一般包括工作广度、深度和（　　）。

A. 完整性

B. 自主性

C. 准确性

D. 反馈性

8. 一份合格、规范的工作说明书必须符合准确性、系统性及（　　）等
要求。

A. 完备性

B. 普遍性

C. 预见性

D. 简约性

E. 特殊性

9. 外部人力资源市场包括（　　　）。

A. 社会市场规模的大小

B. 国家的经济体制

C. 经济结构状况

D. 所有制结构

10. 工作设计的主要内容包括（　　　）。

A. 工作内容

B. 工作职责

C. 工作关系

D. 工作方法

11. 在工作分析时，人力资源部门作为专业部门起到（　　　）的职能。

A. 专业支持

B. 服务

C. 协调

D. 监督

E. 管理

12. 分析人力结构中主管职位与非主管职位，目的在于了解（　　　）。

A. 管理人员的缺口

B. 组织中管理幅度的大小

C. 部门与层次的多少

D. 薪酬成本变化趋势

13. 一份人力资源信息分析报告，主要包括（   ）等内容。

A. 所要分析的问题

B. 分析问题的过程

C. 分析问题的结论

D. 相应的对策措施

14. （   ）是影响人力资源需求预测的内部因素。

A. 企业目标变化

B. 员工素质变化

C. 组织形式变化

D. 企业最高领导层的理念

15. （   ）是内部人力资源供给预测方法。

A. 技能清单法

B. 马尔可夫分析法

C. 管理人员接替计划法

D. 标杆法

16. 岗位设置的几种形式中，通过人力成本来预算的包括（   ）。

A. 基于任务的岗位设置

B. 基于能力的岗位设置

C. 基于团队的岗位设置

D. 以上全是

17. （   ）是组成工作分析小组的成员。

A. 工作分析人员

B. 高层管理人员

C. 直线经理

D. 外部专家和顾问

18. （　　）技能属于通用技能。

A. 计算机使用

B. 外语运用

C. 公文写作

D. 专业技术

19. 在工作分析中，人力资源部的角色包括（　　）。

A. 制订工作分析计划、审核和检查工作流程

B. 对直线经理和任职者培训

C. 起到专业支持、服务和管理的职能

D. 为实施计划建立时间框架

20. 通过（　　）可以激发员工创造力。

A. 工作的广度

B. 工作的深度

C. 工作的完整性

D. 工作的自主性

第二篇
招聘与配置

本篇重点内容：

1. 招聘计划的制订

2. 内外部招聘原则和方法

3. 招聘广告的设计

4. 招聘选拔的方法与流程

5. 人员录用要求和流程

6. 离职面谈的流程

招聘与配置流程：

1. 招聘需求分析（根据人力资源规划和部门发展要求）

2. 招聘计划制订

3. 招聘来源和招聘渠道选择

4. 实施招聘（测试和面试）

5. 人员录用实施（入职条件、薪酬协商、背景调查）

6. 上岗试用（签订劳动合同）

7. **招聘评估**

一、判断题（下列判断正确的请打"√"，错误的打"×"）

1. 招聘计划是组织根据部门发展要求和人力资源规划的人力净需求，工作说明的具体要求，对招聘岗位、人员数量、时间限制等因素做出的详细计划。

（　　）

2. 结合人力资源战略与规划，预测近期人力资源的需求量、类型和趋势是制订招聘计划的前提和依据。

（　　）

3. 招聘计划应由人力资源部门制订，然后由用人部门复核。

（　　）

4. 招聘计划的制订过程包括调研分析、预测和决策三个步骤。

（　　）

5. 招聘计划制订以后，就要执行，不能修改。

（　　）

6. 内部晋升、岗位轮换、临时人员转正等都是内部招聘方法。

（　　）

7. 许多企业在人才招聘过程中出现人才"高消费"现象，如抬高招聘门槛，只招聘本科或研究生以上的人才等，这违反了招聘中的真实客观原则。

（　　）

8. 内部招聘是指组织采用职位公告、岗位竞聘或部门推荐等方式在组织内部招聘新员工。

（　　）

9. 网络招聘又称在线招聘或电子招聘，已经成为越来越多的企业和求职者进行招聘和求职的重要手段。

（　　）

10. 招聘广告的最后部分，要向读者说明投寄申请资料的要求和联系方式，联系方式有三种：通信地址、电子邮件和电话。

（　　）

11. 知识测验作为一种重要的人才甄选方法，可以采用口头表述的方法。

（　　）

12. 知识测验能提高组织人才甄选的效度，有一定预测作用。

（　　）

13. 外部招聘是指根据一定的标准和程序，从组织外部众多应聘者中选拔获取所需人选的方法。

（　　）

14. 招聘调研分析是为了判断未来变化对企业人力资源需求的影响。

（　　）

15. 投射测验注重人格的整体分析，而一般的人格测验往往只能测量某些人格特征。

（　　）

16. 一些调查结果显示，大部分管理职位都是从组织内部提拔起来的人员来担任的。

（　　）

17. 网络广告可以覆盖全部人群，且成本低廉。

（　　）

18. 如果人事部门与用人部门在人选问题上的意见有冲突，应尊重用人部门的意见。

（　　）

19. 仪器人格测评是通过科学的仪器对被试人格进行测试，以了解被试心理获得的一种科学测评方法。

（　　）

20. 组织在招聘中录用能力超出职位要求很多的优秀人才，可以为组织储备人才。

（　　）

21. 一般能力测验即通常所说的智力测验。

（　　）

22. 一般能力测验，一般只能对个别被测试者进行。

（　　）

23. 当要将招聘限定于某一区域，或可能的求职者集中于某一区域时，可通过杂志招聘的方式进行招聘。

（　　）

24. 招聘人员的形象、谈吐、待人接物等方面也很重要，因为这能反映出该组织成员素质的培养和人格的塑造，是外部招聘的一个重要环节。

（　　）

25. 结构化面试中，面试的内容在面试之前已经形成一个固定的框架（或问题清单），主考官根据框架对每个应聘者分别做相同的提问。

（　　）

26. 结构化面试适用于单独的中高级管理人员面试。

（　　）

27. 知识测验试卷不仅用来考察应聘者的知识和能力，同时还是组织形象和业务水平的体现。

（　　）

28. 传统面试的一个突出问题是考官的提问太随意，想问什么就问什么；

同时评价也缺少客观依据，想怎么评就怎么评。

（　　）

29. 合格的面试官应具备的主要特征包括客观、公正、丰富的社会经验和熟练运用各种面试技巧。

（　　）

30. 客观题能给应聘者很大的自由度，能够看出应聘者的综合能力和思维深度。

（　　）

31. 人格测验主要包括态度、兴趣、动机和性格等的测验。

（　　）

32. 以工作分析为基础确定测评要素是结构化面试的重要特点。

（　　）

33. 在面试的中间环节，需要遵循 STAR 原则，其中 T 是指时间。

（　　）

34. 当组织出现职位空缺时，应首选外部招聘。

（　　）

35. 通过人才交流中心选择人员，适用于急需招聘和长期招聘的职位。

（　　）

36. 管理职位或关键职位招聘可采用两轮面试，即初试和复试，是一种非压力的一对一面试。

（　　）

37. 在录用决策时，当最终人选多于所要录用的人员时，应遵循重工作能力、优先求职动机、价值观认同等原则。

（　　）

38. 结构化面试是指面试的内容、方式、评委构成、程序、评分标准等构成要素，按统一制定的标准和要求进行的面试。

（　　）

39. 引起歧视的因素主要有：一些不合理的招工条件，如年龄、是否已婚等，以及过分注重人员的学历和工作经验，而对于其创新能力、管理能力等没有进行充分评价等。

（　　）

40. 优秀的应聘者非常抢手，因此在确保决策质量的前提下，要尽快做出录用决策。

（　　）

41. 录用决策的一般原则是"谁用人谁决策"，遵循少而精的原则。

（　　）

42. 录用决策一旦做出，就应该立即通知被录用者。

（　　）

43. 组织的人才储备通常分为内储和外储两种，内储就是暂时把预留人才储存在组织内部。

（　　）

44. 新员工培训的目的在于将组织录用的人员由社会人转变为组织人。

（　　）

45. 人员的录用决策按照决策过程的实施可分为过关淘汰式、汇总评估式、混合式。

（　　）

46. 招聘面试的 STAR 原则包括情景、任务、行动和结果。

（　　）

47. 同一用人单位与同一劳动者只能约定一次试用期。

（　　）

48. 劳动合同期限 3 个月以上不满 1 年的，试用期不得超过 1 个月。

（　　）

49. 劳动合同期限 1 年以上不满 3 年的，试用期不得超过 3 个月。

（　　）

50. 3 年以上固定期限和无固定期限的劳动合同，试用期不得超过 6 个月。

（　　）

51. 单轮测试决策尤其适用于校园招聘。

（　　）

52. 员工录用是招聘的目的和成果。在招聘考核中选拔出来的合格人员，只有办理一定手续，才能成为组织员工。录用手续的办理是确定员工身份的依据。

（　　）

53. 人员配置过程包括招聘、选拔、雇佣这几个关键的要素，同时还包含了人员流动过程中发生的步骤和活动。

（　　）

54. 人员配置是为了创造组织效能而从事的获取、运用和留任足够质量和数量劳动力队伍的过程。

（　　）

55. 人员晋升是指员工在职位上的横向发展，是一种特殊的人员调配方式。

（　　）

56. 人员配置的主要类型有人员调配和岗位轮换。

（　　）

57. 对有价值的离职员工做最后挽留是离职面谈的目的之一。

（　　）

58. 录用决策体现择优录用原则，这是人员录用的核心。

（　　）

59. 霍兰德的职业性向理论认为，每个人的性格和天赋决定了其职业性向，职业性向（包括价值观、动机和需要等）是决定一个人职业选择的重要因素。

（　　）

60. 心理测验是通过对人的一组可观测的样本行为进行系统的测量来推断人的心理特征的测验方法。

（　　）

二、单项选择题（下列每题的选项中，只有 1 个是正确的）

1. 招聘调研分析主要调研两方面内容：一是根据组织发展和运行状况，明确工作任务及完成这些任务所需人员状况，二是（　　）。

A. 分析本组织整体人力资源或者局部人力资源状况

B. 分析本组织人力资源规划及当前的工作任务情况

C. 确定如何开展招聘工作

D. 确定招聘的范围、数量和规模等情况

2. 招聘计划的制订过程包括调研分析、预测和（　　）。

A. 选择

B. 决策

C. 沟通

D. 确认

3. 招聘广告设计原则应符合 AIDAM 原则，其中"I"的意思是（　　）。

A. 引起注意

B. 产生兴趣

C. 激发愿望

D. 采取行动

4. 招聘广告中岗位要求的主要内容可以用"KASO"概括，（　　）不包含在其中。

A. 知识

B. 能力

C. 技巧

D. 机会

5. 招聘广告中可以不提供的联系方式是（　　）。

A. 传真

B. 公司地址

C. 电子邮箱

D. 电话

6. 在招聘广告的内容方面，美国学者戈登（J. Gordon）、威尔逊（P. Wilson）和斯旺（H. Swan）在1982年通过对报纸读者的调查来了解企业招聘广告中各种信息的必要性，其中（　　）的必要性最高。

A. 工作地点

B. 工资

C. 工作经历

D. 岗位职责

7. （　　）不是外部招聘的原则。

A. 公正公平原则

B. 适用适合原则

C. 合理配置原则

D. 真实客观原则

E. 沟通与服务原则

8. （　　　）不是心理测验的特点。

A. 间接性

B. 绝对性

C. 相对性

D. 客观性

9. "STAR" 原则中的 "S" 意思是（　　　）。

A. 具体

B. 合适

C. 情景

D. 选择

10. （　　　）是世界上最早的智力量表。

A. 自陈式量表

B. 比奈—西蒙量表

C. MBTI 工作风格测验

D. 仪器人格测评

11. 投射测验也称投射技术，最早由（　　　）提出。

A. 卡特尔

B. Frank

C. 卡尔·荣格

D. 霍兰德

12. 下面关于投射测验的描述，（　　　）是不正确的。

A. 呈现给被试者的是一个模糊而相对无结构的刺激情景

B. 被试者知道测验的目的，因此反应具有针对性

C. 被试者可以用各种方式来自由回答问题

D. 注重人格的整体分析

13. 一些调查结果显示，高达90%的管理岗位都是由（　　）获得的。

A. 外部招聘

B. 内部招聘

C. 猎头

D. 内部竞聘

14. 内部招聘的信息覆盖面应是（　　）。

A. 有关部门员工

B. 后备人选库中的员工

C. 整个组织内部的全体员工

D. 公司和部门领导推荐的人员

15. 结构化面试的主要缺点是（　　）。

A. 不能减少考官评价的主观性

B. 不能控制面试的时间

C. 不能有效进行应聘者的比较

D. 不能根据应聘者的不同特点提出针对性的问题

16. 在结构化面试中，考官的人数必须在（　　）人以上。

A. 2

B. 3

C. 4

D. 5

17. 无论是通过选拔优秀的员工到更高的职位上工作，还是通过考试将员工安排到更适合他的岗位上去，都应当让广大员工认识到，不断地提高自己

的工作能力将会在组织内获得更大的发展空间，这体现了内部招聘的（　　）原则。

A. 机会均等

B. 任人唯贤，唯才是用

C. 合理配置，用人所长

D. 激励

18.（　　）能提高组织人才甄选的效度。

A. 知识测验

B. 心理测验

C. 能力测验

D. 智力测验

19.（　　）所问的问题具有最高的一致性和标准性。

A. 间接面试

B. 情境面试

C. 结构面试

D. 非结构面试

20. 下面关于知识测验表述错误的是（　　）。

A. 采取书面试卷或者面试的形式

B. 可以大规模进行

C. 成本相对较低

D. 可能出现"高分低能"现象

21. 对于管理人员，包括关键岗位，一般由（　　）批准后录取。

A. 部门经理

B. 人力资源经理

C. 总经理

D. 招聘经理

22. 某公司在其内部刊物上发布了 6 个岗位的招聘通知，这属于（　　　）。

A. 推荐法

B. 内部竞聘法

C. 档案法

D. 中介法

23. 面试中，面试官接连问了如下问题：

①能不能分享一下你作为领导组织一个团队完成一项具有挑战性任务的

例子？

②当时的情况是怎样的？想要达成什么样的目标？

③你作为领导是怎么做的？

④结果怎么样？

该面试官遵循了（　　　）原则。

A. MBTI

B. DISC

C. STAR

D. SMART

24. （　　　）体现人岗匹配原则。

A. 录用流程

B. 员工安置

C. 录用决策

D. 招聘选拔

25. （　　　）录用人才虽然有自身缺陷，但总体来说，是目前最为公正合

理、行之有效的甄选人才的方法之一。

A. 知识测验

B. 能力测验

C. 心理测验

D. 人格测验

26. 下列哪一个录用招聘程序是科学的（　　）。

　A. 人力资源部初步筛选，高层经理和招聘专员测试，最后进行匹配度分析

　B. 业务部门初步筛选，人力资源部考察测试，再到高层经理和招聘专员测试，最后进行匹配度分析

　C. 人力资源部初步筛选，业务部门考察测试，最后进行匹配度分析

　D. 人力资源部初步筛选，业务部门考察测试，高层经理和招聘专员测试，最后进行匹配度分析

27. 非压力面试一般用于招聘（　　）。

　A. 普通职位人员

　B. 管理人员

　C. 财务人员

　D. 高级管理人员

28. （　　）不作为面试官应具备的基本特征。

　A. 良好的个人品格和修养，为人正直

　B. 丰富的社会工作经验

　C. 善于把握人际关系

　D. 外表气质出众

29. 心理测验只能测量人的外显行为，即通过测量个体对测验题目的反应，从而推论其心理素质，体现了心理测验的（　　）。

　A. 间接性

　B. 相对性

C. 客观性

D. 可变性

30. 在对人的行为作比较时，没有一个绝对的零点，即没有绝对的标准，有的只是一个连续尺度上的行为序列。测量就是看每个人处在这个序列上的什么位置，这体现了心理测验的（   ）。

A. 间接性

B. 相对性

C. 客观性

D. 可变性

31. 某企业在招聘时，只注重应聘人员的学历和工作经验，而对于其创新能力、管理能力等并没有进行充分评价。这违背了人员配置的（   ）原则。

A. 计划

B. 科学

C. 公平

D. 动态

32. 通知应聘者是录用工作的一个重要部分，通知包括录用通知和（   ）。

A. 聘任协议

B. 报到通知

C. 离职程序

D. 辞谢通知

33. （   ）的测量效度、信度都比较高，比较适合规模较大，组织、规范性较强的录用面试。

A. 行为面试

B. 半结构化面试

C. 结构化面试

D. 非结构化面试

34. （   ）录用决策不是按照决策周期划分的。

A. 过关淘汰式

B. 汇总评估式

C. 混合式

D. 单轮决策式

35. 录用项目开发人员时，若应聘者缺乏创新开拓的能力，则不管该应聘者其他能力如何，都不会被录用。这是采用了（   ）录用决策模型。

A. 补偿型

B. 非补偿型

C. 混合模型

D. 汇总评估式

36. （   ）又称问卷法，即对拟测量的个性特征编制若干测题（陈述句），被试者逐项给出书面答案，依据其答案来测量评价某项个性特征。

A. 自陈式量表法

B. 投射测验

C. 仪器人格测评

D. MBTI 工作风格测验

37. 基于如下假设：个体不是被动地接受外界的刺激，而是主动地、有选择地给外界刺激赋予某种意义，然后，表现出适当的反应，人们可以从这些反应中推论他的人格（   ）。

A. 自陈式量表法

B. 投射测验

C. 仪器人格测评

D. MBTI 工作风格测验

38. 如签订两年劳动合同，则可以约定试用期（　　）。

A. 1 个月

B. 2 个月

C. 3 个月

D. 6 个月

39.（　　）是建立在系统有序基础上的内部职位空缺补充办法。

A. 内部举荐

B. 内部竞聘

C. 内部晋升

D. 上级输送

40. 劳动合同中不得约定试用期的情形是（　　）。

A. 劳动合同期限不满 3 个月

B. 无固定期限劳动合同

C. 1 年以上劳动合同

D. 3 年以上劳动合同

41. "金无足赤，人无完人"说明人员配置时，要遵循（　　）原理，达到"1 + 1 > 2"的效果。

A. 个人与团队匹配

B. 个人与组织匹配

C. 个人与岗位匹配

D. 能力与岗位匹配

42. 某企业在招聘时，只注重应聘人员的学历和工作经验，而对于其创新能力、管理能力等并没有进行充分评价。这违背了人员配置的（　　）原则。

A. 计划

B. 科学

C. 公平

D. 动态

43. "人尽其才"体现了人员录用中的（   ）。

A. 公平竞争原则

B. 择优录用原则

C. 人岗匹配原则

D. 符合法律原则

44. （   ）对整个面试程序、考官结构、评价标准等都进行了严格规定。

A. 非结构化面试

B. 半结构化面试

C. 结构化面试

D. 情景式面试

45. 下面关于投射测验描述不正确的是（   ）。

A. 呈现给被试者的是一个模糊而相对无结构的刺激情景

B. 被试者知道测验的目的，因此反应具有针对性

C. 被试者可以用各种方式来自由回答问题

D. 注重人格的整体分析

46. （   ）是尽量减少人员流失和规避相关人事纠纷及法律风险的一种方法。

A. 系统的员工培训

B. 科学的绩效管理

C. 规范的入职管理

D. 规范的离职管理

47. 在人员录用时，应遵循（   ）程序。

A. 制定录用制度→做出录用决策→办理录用手续→签订劳动合同

B. 制定录用制度→办理录用手续→做出录用决策→签订劳动合同

C. 做出录用决策→制定录用制度→办理录用手续→签订劳动合同

D. 制定录用制度→做出录用决策→签订劳动合同→办理录用手续

48.（   ）即通过公开考试、公平竞争、择优录用，广泛地选择优秀人才的任用制度。

A. 选任制

B. 委任制

C. 聘任制

D. 考任制

49. 离职面谈一般由（   ）进行。

A. 人力资源部

B. 部门主管

C. 公司总经理

D. 团队负责人

50. 新员工培训的目的在于将组织录用的人员由（   ）。

A. 经济人转变为社会人

B. 经济人转变为组织人

C. 社会人转变为组织人

D. 社会人转变为经济人

51. 如果待招聘人员是在人员预算范围外，需要（   ）对招聘的必要性进行审核和论证。

A. 人力资源经理

B. 部门经理

C. 公司高层管理人员

D. 用人部门

52. 如企业要招聘某一领域的专业人才时,可采用(   )。

A. 校园招聘

B. 人才招聘会

C. 网络招聘

D. 专业杂志

53. 职业适应性测验,有时也称为动力测验,它关注人对从事某项活动或职业的一种内在倾向,其理论基础是(   )。

A. 韦氏量表

B. 霍兰德的职业性向理论

C. 九型人格

D. 卡特尔人格因素测验

54. 如果判断某一人在某一专业或职业活动中表现出来的能力,或者测定在工作中成功和适应的可能性,我们应该采取(   )手段。

A. 智力测验

B. 能力倾向测验

C. 认知测验

D. 心理运动测验

55. 根据应聘者所有测试的总成绩做出录用决策,称为(   )。

A. 过关淘汰式

B. 汇总评估式

C. 混合式

D. 单轮决策式

56. "你之前在哪里工作?"是面试实施时(   )涉及的问题。

A. 关系建立阶段

B. 导入阶段

C. 正题阶段

D. 深入阶段

57. 企业人才晋升必须遵循以下原则，但（　　）除外。

A. 德才兼备、选贤任能的原则

B. 机会均等、用人所长的原则

C. 保密原则

D. 有系统、有计划的原则

58. （　　）尤其适用于校园招聘。

A. 过关淘汰决策法

B. 混合式决策法

C. 单轮测试决策法

D. 汇总评估决策法

59. 从"金无足赤，人无完人"可以看出，企业在人员配置时，必须遵循（　　）原理。

A. 个人与岗位匹配

B. 个人与团队匹配

C. 个人与组织匹配

D. 个人与环境匹配

60. 面试考官培训是为了改变传统面试中凭经验和直觉评价的问题，通过面试的准确性，面试培训一般包括理论知识和（　　）。

A. 业务知识

B. 实践技巧

C. 公司文化

D. 职业素养

三、多项选择题（下列每题的选项中，至少有 2 个是正确的）

1. 招聘计划的制订过程包括（　　　）。

A. 调研分析

B. 预测

C. 决策

D. 确认

2. 内部招聘的渠道有（　　　）。

A. 内部晋升或岗位轮换

B. 内部竞聘

C. 内部员工举荐

D. 临时人员转正

3. 外部招聘应遵循以下基本原则，包括（　　　）。

A. 公正公平原则

B. 适用适合原则

C. 真实客观原则

D. 沟通与服务原则

4. 知识试题编制要符合的要求是（　　　）。

A. 试题表述规范，语言没有歧义

B. 试题难度要大有利于区分应聘者能力

C. 主观题目与客观题目相结合

D. 试题涉及知识点与要考察的岗位要求相关

E. 试题题量安排合适

5. 心理测验对员工招聘的意义（　　　）。

A. 提高组织人才甄选的效度

B. 导向作用

C. 降低招聘成本，起到优胜劣汰的作用

D. 提高招聘效率，实现批量测评

6. 内部招聘应遵循（　　　）基本原则。

A. 机会均等

B. 任人唯贤，唯才是用

C. 沟通与服务

D. 激励员工

E. 合理配置

7. 为实现人员配置的有效性，需遵循（　　　）基本原则。

A. 公平原则

B. 动态原则

C. 计划原则

D. 科学原则

8. 离职面谈要了解的信息包括（　　　）。

A. 对所在部门需要改进的问题的合理化建议

B. 离职人员对公司战略愿景的评价

C. 离职后个人职业生涯规划

D. 对公司当前工作环境以及内部人际关系的看法

E. 离职人员离职的真实原因

9. （　　　）是人员录用的原则。

A. 录用流程体现公平竞争原则

B. 录用决策体现择优录用原则

C. 员工安置体现人岗匹配的原则

D. 劳动关系体现符合法律的原则

10. 员工离职的组织内部原因有（　　）。

A. 职业发展空间不足

B. 无法达到岗位能力要求

C. 与领导关系不好

D. 有竞争对手挖墙脚

E. 薪酬福利不佳

11. 进行外部招聘时，招聘人员应真实、客观地向应聘者介绍组织的情况，其好处是（　　）。

A. 提高工作满意度

B. 防止人员流动率过高

C. 提高招聘的有效性

D. 提高工作期望和工作激情

12. 人岗匹配具体包括（　　）方面。

A. 气质、性格与岗位的匹配

B. 能力与组织的匹配

C. 能力与岗位的匹配

D. 价值观、兴趣与岗位的匹配

13. 有关录用要求表述不准确的是（　　）。

A. 优秀的应聘者非常抢手，应该在确保决策质量的前提下，尽快做出录用决策

B. 参与录用决策的人数越多越好，可以从多角度分析，这样能对决策质量的提高有帮助

C. 如果急需用人的话，可以适当降低标准

D. 录用招聘程序要一个层次一个层次有序地进行

E. 对于一般基层人员，由人力资源部主管单独决定即可

14. 一个人在经过选拔评价并且各项胜任力都符合职位和组织的要求后，要能够进入该组织工作，还要符合以下条件（　　　）。

A. 从原雇主处辞职

B. 将人事档案转移到组织指定的档案管理机构

C. 体检合格

D. 签订劳动合同

15. 人员的录用决策按照决策周期的安排可分为（　　　）。

A. 单轮测试决策

B. 过关淘汰式

C. 汇总评估式

D. 混合式

16. 结构化面试的优点包括（　　　）。

A. 使所有的应聘者感到公平

B. 使外界感受到组织招聘的公开、公正和公平

C. 使面试官以较统一的标准，衡量和比较不同的应聘者

D. 操作简便，使面试顺利进行

17. 员工晋升的方式有（　　　）。

A. 选任制

B. 委任制

C. 聘任制

D. 考任制

E. 阶梯制

18. 下面哪一类情况不得约定试用期（　　　）。

A. 以完成一定工作任务为期限的劳动合同

B. 劳动合同期限不满 3 个月的

C. 劳动合同期限不满 6 个月的

D. 稀缺人才

19. 一般能力是完成各种活动都必须具备的某种能力，主要包括(　　)。

A. 绘画能力

B. 记忆能力

C. 音乐能力

D. 注意力

E. 想象能力

20. 面试评价时，一般采用（　　）评价方法。

A. 打分式评价

B. 口语式评价

C. 评语式评价

D. 综合式评价

第三篇
培训与开发

本篇重点内容：

1. 培训需求分析的方法和流程

2. 培训计划的内容和编制

3. 培训方法的选择及注意事项

4. 培训师资和培训机构的选择方法和注意事项

5. 培训预算编制

培训与开发流程：

1. 培训需求分析

2. 培训计划制订

3. 培训组织实施

4. 培训效果评估

5. 培训总结反馈

一、判断题（下列判断正确的请打"√"，错误的打"×"）

1. 培训需求分析是培训的首要工作，是整个培训有效进行的前提，也是制订培训计划的基础。

（　）

2. 培训需求分析主要由两部分工作组成：培训需求调查和调查结果分析。

（　）

3. 任务分析最终的结果决定了培训对象。

（　）

4. 在进行任务分析时，任务的重要性是对员工完成这项任务的能力要求，一定程度上反映从事此项任务的门槛高度。

（　）

5. 绩效分析法的适用范围有限，不适用于那些复杂程度高的工作。

（　）

6. 相对于组织分析和任务分析，人员分析可以采取的方法更为广泛。

（　）

7. 企业要求具备的理想状态与现实状态之间的差距，就是培训需求。

（　）

8. 企业完全可以通过企业现存的书面资料进行培训需求分析。

（　）

9. 在制订培训计划时，要充分考虑到人力资源开发的需要为人才储备做好基础性工作。

（　）

10. 保证人力资源开发系统的有效性是培训需求分析的作用之一。

（　　）

11. 人员分析的关键就是找出哪些人员"不愿"，哪些人员"不能"，这样才能有针对性地设计培训方案。

（　　）

12. 实行扩张投资战略的公司会比实行其他战略的公司更看重诸如新职业介绍和寻找工作技能方面的培训。

（　　）

13. 从培训需求分析到培训实施、再到培训效果评估，是一个随时与员工沟通的过程。

（　　）

14. 任务分析的最终成果就是对任务活动的详细描述，主要内容包括员工执行的任务和完成任务所需要的技术、技能、能力和态度，即 KSAO。

（　　）

15. 所谓培训目标的标准要素是指在什么条件下要达到规定的标准。

（　　）

16. 对于没有战略目标理念的公司，培训支出及培训频率一般都要低于期望通过培训实现企业战略目标的公司。

（　　）

17. 研究表明，同事和管理者对培训开发的支持，在员工参与培训开发的热情和动力方面有一定的帮助。

（　　）

18. 培训目标是指培训活动的目的和预期效果。

（　　）

19. 培训目标的内容要素包括知识的传授、技能的培养等。　（　　）

20. 任务分析通常要优先于组织分析和人员分析。

（　　　）

21. 组织战略在一定程度上决定了培训的方向和方式。

（　　　）

22. 问卷调查法的主要问题是：对问卷设计的要求较高，被调查者很少有发挥的空间，很难发现新的和更深层面的信息，可能出现低返回率的情况。

（　　　）

23. 访谈法操作简单，可以在大范围内开展。

（　　　）

24. 培训目标是制订员工培训计划的直接依据也是培训评估的重要依据。

（　　　）

25. 投资回报率指培训的货币收益与培训成本的比较，可用来评价组织培训的效益。

（　　　）

26. 培训预算是培训的基本保障，是领导者审批培训计划的重要因素。

（　　　）

27. 工作轮换是传统培训方法中"模拟式"培训方法。

（　　　）

28. 师徒制属于"在岗培训式"培训方法之一。

（　　　）

29. 在选择培训方法时，要把培训时间的考量放在第一位。

（　　　）

30. 培训计划必须满足组织和员工两方面的需求，充分考虑人才培养的超前性和培训结果的不确定性。

（　　　）

31. 培训对象在完成培训后应该表现出的行为、行为赖以发生的特定环境条件和组织可以接受的业绩标准，称为培训目标。

（　　）

32. 对于长期培训计划而言，时间过长则对有些变数无法做出预测，时间过短就失去了长期培训计划的意义。

（　　）

33. 培训方法的选择与培训经费无关。

（　　）

34. 为外部培训师配备助手，能较好地解决外部培训师对组织不了解，导致培训针对性差的问题。

（　　）

35. 企业每年会有大量不同内容的培训，在企业缺乏高质量的培训师资或外包培训成本更低、效益更好时，组织倾向于向外购买培训服务。

（　　）

36. 培训师的选择是培训工作取得成功的关键，也是培训准备工作的重中之重。

（　　）

37. 培训预算包括：场地费，食宿费，培训器材、教材费，培训相关人员工资及外聘老师讲课费和交通差旅费。

（　　）

38. 费用总额法是有些企业实行划定人力资源部门全年的费用总额，费用总额包括招聘费用、培训费用、体检费用等人力资源部门全年所有费用。

（　　）

39. 培训师的来源主要有两个，一是来自组织内部，二是来自组织外部。

（　　）

40. 只有对组织的使命有较深刻的理解，才能使培训需求分析做到有针对性和目标性。

（　　）

41. 为了减少预算时间，应由培训部门独立完成预算编制任务。

（　　）

42. 预先确定企业内人均培训预算额，然后再乘以在职人员数量的培训预算确定法，被称为费用总额法。

（　　）

43. 成本统计专家指出，一位一线工人的工资是其创造价值的1/3。

（　　）

44. 制订短期培训计划时需要着重考虑的两个要素是可操作性和效果。

（　　）

45. 企业中期培训计划可有可无。

（　　）

46. 短期培训计划是指时间跨度在1年以内的培训计划。

（　　）

47. 根据培训师的知识和经验、培训技能、个人魅力三个维度，以及其一般和好两种表现，可以将培训师从高到低分为八种类型。

（　　）

48. 一些相关但价值不大的内容罗列在一起，以求丰富培训内容，是企业在组织培训活动中常犯的错误之一。

（　　）

49. 培训机构的选择步骤包括：确定培训目标，与培训机构联系发出征询建议书，进行挑选，最终确定。

（　　）

50. 培训是一个帮助人学习的过程，培训师在教学中始终处于领导地位。

（　　）

51. 内部培训师的来源一般为各级管理人员和各职类职种的业务骨干。

（　　）

52. 聘用外部培训师的一个最大问题是培训工作中的沟通和协调相对比较困难。

（　　）

53. 比较外部培训和内部培训，企业内部培训是企业培训发展的方向。

（　　）

54. 在每个预算年度开始时，将所有在进行的管理活动都看成重新开始，即以零为基础，根据组织目标重新审查每项活动对实现组织目标的意义和效果，并在成本收益分析基础上，重新排出各项管理活动的优先顺序，是需求预算法。

（　　）

55. 内部培训师制度也是一种有效的激励手段。

（　　）

56. 新技术培训可以避免员工的时间与培训项目日程安排发生冲突。

（　　）

57. 培训对象在不同区域且培训交通费用较高时，通常采用在训培训等新技术培训方法。

（　　）

58. 对于技术类培训，培训预算应该集中在企业骨干技术人员身上。

（　　）

59. 企业一般都会将培训预算向企业高级经理和骨干员工倾斜，这样做是合适的。

（　　）

二、单项选择题（下列每题的选项中，只有 1 个是正确的）

1. 任务的重要性一般，但任务水平要求高，说明可（　　）。

A. 不去培训

B. 及时培训

C. 选择培训

D. 重点培训

2. 在进行任务分析时，必须明确两个主要因素，即任务的重要性与（　　）。

A. 可行性

B. 科学性

C. 水平

D. 标准

3. 下面说法正确的是（　　）。

A. 组织分析先于任务分析、人员分析

B. 任务分析先于组织分析、人员分析

C. 人员分析先于任务分析、组织分析

D. 组织分析、任务分析、人员分析同时进行

4. （　　）的基本目标是确认差距。

A. 培训需求分析

B. 培训计划制订

C. 培训考核

D. 培训评估

5. 任务分析过程中，（   ）非常重要。

A. 分析

B. 沟通

C. 观察

D. 方法

6. 厘清工作绩效令人不满意的原因，是知识、技术、能力的欠缺，还是属于个人动机或工作设计方面问题，是（   ）要解决的问题。

A. 组织分析

B. 岗位分析

C. 人员分析

D. 任务分析

7. 在培训需求分析过程中，当调查对象规模大，时间和资金相对有限时，（   ）是值得推荐的方法。

A. 访谈法

B. 观察法

C. 调查问卷法

D. 关键事件法

8. 使用资料档案收集法进行培训需求分析时，必须注意的是（   ）。

A. 书面资料只是一方面的信息，而不是全部

B. 翻阅尽可能多的档案

C. 搜集尽可能多的信息

D. 不用进行分析直接应用

9. （   ）不属于企业培训与开发的目标。

A. 态度改变

B. 知识掌握

C. 增加福利

D. 业绩提升

10. 企业一般会将培训预算向（   ）倾斜。

A. 企业高级经理和骨干员工

B. 企业高级经理和普通员工

C. 骨干员工和普通员工

D. 核心员工和普通员工

11. 培训成果的类别包括（   ）大类。

A. 2

B. 3

C. 4

D. 5

12. （   ）关系到某项工作的具体任务、行为及行为发生的频率。

A. 任务水平

B. 任务数量

C. 质量

D. 任务重要性

13. （   ）是任务分析的步骤。

①列出要执行任务的基本清单

②确定要分析的工作岗位

③明确要胜任各项任务需要的知识、技术和能力

④采用书面调查等访问形式获取信息

A. ①—②—③—④

B. ②—①—③—④

C. ①—③—②—④

D. ②—①—④—③

14. 任务分析的最终成果就是对任务活动的详细描述，主要内容包括员工执行的任务和完成任务需要的知识、技能、能力和其他素质，即（   ）。

A. KSAO

B. AIDA

C. STAR

D. MBTI

15. （   ）的关键就是找出哪些人员"不愿"，哪些人员"不能"，这样才能有针对性地设计培训方案。

A. 组织分析

B. 任务分析

C. 人员分析

D. 绩效分析

16. （   ）通常是同时进行的。

A. 组织分析和任务分析

B. 组织分析和人员分析

C. 任务分析和人员分析

D. 组织分析、任务分析和人员分析

17. 确定重要的任务及需要在培训开发中加以强调的知识、技能和行为方式以帮助员工完成任务，是（   ）要解决的问题。

A. 组织层面

B. 战略层面

C. 任务层面

D. 人员层面

18. 评价员工在技术或技能运用，以及行为方式上的提高程度，是培训成果中的（　　）。

A. 认知成果

B. 绩效成果

C. 技能成果

D. 投资回报率

19. 衡量员工对培训内容中原理、事实、技术、程序或过程的熟悉程度，是培训成果中的（　　）。

A. 认知成果

B. 绩效成果

C. 技能成果

D. 投资回报率

20. 培训目标一般包括内容要素、（　　）和条件要素。

A. 人员要素

B. 战略要素

C. 标准要素

D. 结果要素

21. 制订培训计划必须以（　　）为依据。

A. 企业发展计划

B. 部门工作计划

C. 培训需求

D. 内部资源分配

22. 以提高员工分析和决策能力、书面和口头沟通能力、人际关系技巧能力等为主要内容的培训属于（　　）。

A. 技能培训

B. 知识传授培训

C. 态度转变培训

D. 工作方法改进培训

23.（　　）不属于人力资源部门在培训和开发工作中的责任。

A. 提供行政上的监控

B. 培训计划的编制

C. 培训资源上的保证

D. 培训成本控制

24.（　　）是用来衡量员工对培训项目的感性认识，包括个人态度、动机、忍耐力、价值观等在内的情感、心理因素的变化情况，这些因素通常影响或决定个人的行为意向。

A. 认知成果

B. 绩效成果

C. 技能成果

D. 投资回报率

25. 培训需求分析中，（　　）可以让较多的员工参与培训的决策，因而具有更多的沟通、倾诉和激励作用，同时也可能意见分散，而且与组织动作没有太大的关系。

A. 问卷调查法

B. 访谈法

C. 观察法

D. 头脑风暴法

26. 在以下几种培训需求方法中，（　　）的成本相对较低。

A. 观察法

B. 问卷调查法

C. 访谈法

D. 头脑风暴法

27. 组织期望员工以什么样的标准来做这件事情，是培训目标的(　　　)。

A. 内容要素

B. 标准要素

C. 条件要素

D. 结果要素

28. (　　　) 是指培训活动的目的和预期效果。

A. 培训内容

B. 培训目标

C. 培训结果

D. 培训计划

29. 中期培训计划是指时间跨度为 (　　　) 的培训计划。

A. 1～3 年

B. 3～5 年

C. 小于 1 年

D. 大于 5 年

30. (　　　) 适用于那些能够通过观察加以了解的工作，不适用于那些复杂程度高的工作。

A. 面谈法

B. 观察法

C. 工作任务分析法

D. 调查问卷法

31. 受训员工的流动率、事故发生率、成本、产量、质量、顾客服务水平等指标的上升或下降情况，是培训成果中的（　　）。

A. 认知成果

B. 绩效成果

C. 感情成果

D. 投资回报率

32. 如果采用在岗培训的方法，则会出现生产力浪费。专家们估计，在岗培训时所浪费的生产力是正常生产时的（　　）倍。

A. 1

B. 2

C. 3

D. 4

33. 如果培训学习资料的内容绝大多数以事实为依据，那最好采用的培训方式为（　　）。

A. 课堂讲授

B. 在职培训

C. 情景模拟

D. 案例研究

34. （　　）是培训的基本保障，是领导者审批培训计划的重要因素。

A. 培训目标

B. 培训预算

C. 培训方法

D. 培训内容

35. 在培训中，改变员工态度的训练方法宜采用（　　）和角色扮演。

A. 行为模拟

B. 感受训练

C. 工作轮换

D. 活动游戏式

36. 当公司进行年末总结和下一年度计划时，应该由（　　）确定培训预算的投放原则和培训方针，以保证培训预算"名正言顺"和"钱出有因"。

A. 公司高层领导

B. 人力资源部经理

C. 提出培训的部门负责人

D. 第三方机构

37. 培训组织实施主要包括培训方法的选择、培训师的选择、培训机构的选择和（　　）。

A. 培训需求分析

B. 制订培训计划

C. 培训预算的编制

D. 确定培训目标

38. 只有尽可能地在预算程序中吸引更多的人参与，才能更有效地把握公司业务规划和真正的培训需求，从而保证培训预算切实支持公司战略业务发展和员工个人职业生涯发展，是（　　）要求。

A. 准确性原则

B. 合作原则

C. 速度原则

D. 合理原则

39. 在选择培训方法时，要把（　　）的考量放在第一位。

A. 培训内容

B. 培训目标

C. 培训师资

D. 培训评估

40.（　　）的选择在培训过程中至关重要，直接关系到培训工作的成败。

A. 培训内容

B. 培训方法

C. 培训对象

D. 培训地点

41.（　　）可以解决外部培训师培训针对性差的问题。

A. 增加讲课费

B. 封闭培训

C. 配备助手

D. 增加培训时间

42. 承袭上年度的经费，再加上一定比例的变动，是培训预算编制的（　　）。

A. 比例预算法

B. 承袭预算法

C. 比较预算法

D. 费用总额法

43.（　　）是机会成本。

A. 场地费

B. 食宿费

C. 教材费

D. 学员参加培训而耽误工作所花费的成本

44. 培训需求分析是确定培训目标，设计培训的前提，也是进行（　　）的基础。

A. 培训评估

B. 培训实施

C. 培训管理

D. 培训总结

45. 长期培训计划一般是指时间跨度为（　　　）以上的培训计划。

A. 1 ~ 2 年

B. 2 ~ 3 年

C. 3 ~ 5 年

D. 5 年以上

46. 刚毕业的大学生到不同部门工作以丰富其工作经验，从而确定其长处和弱点的培训方式为（　　　）。

A. 岗前培训

B. 工作轮换

C. 行动学习

D. 在职培训

47. 确定培训预算时，核算方法简单、核算成本低，很多企业都采用（　　　）。

A. 比例预算法

B. 零基预算法

C. 比较预算法

D. 需求预算法

48. 培训主管部门要争取和发动从领导到广大员工的参与和有效合作，让培训真正发挥效果、产生效益，是（　　　）要求。

A. 准确性原则

B. 合作原则

C. 速度原则

D. 合理原则

49.（　　）是培训预算工作的第一要点。

A. 培训预算分配

B. 统计培训对象信息

C. 确定内外训比例

D. 培训地点选择

50. 需要进行岗前培训的员工不包括（　　）。

A. 新入职员工

B. 晋升的员工

C. 轮岗的员工

D. 核心员工

51. 培训需求分析的基本目标是（　　）。

A. 做好工作预测

B. 提出培训要求

C. 确认差距

D. 编制培训制度

52. 培训需求的组织分析主要是通过对组织的战略导向、组织资源和

（　　）进行分析。

A. 组织氛围

B. 组织人员数量

C. 组织人员质量

D. 组织薪酬情况

53. 企业一般会将培训预算向高级经理和（　　）倾斜。

A. 基层员工

B. 骨干员工

C. 新员工

D. 普通员工

54. 短期培训计划是指时间跨度为（　　　）的培训计划。

A. 半年内

B. 1 年内

C. 1～2 年

D. 2～3 年

55. （　　）不是培训预算的原则。

A. 速度原则

B. 准确性原则

C. 合作原则

D. 导向原则

56. （　　）可以在短期内提高内部培训师的授课水平。

A. 做外部资深培训师的助手

B. 参加内部培训

C. 参加外部培训

D. 模拟授课，小组交流

57. 公司根据同行业培训预算的平均值确定一年度的培训预算，我们将这种方法称之为（　　　）。

A. 推算法

B. 需求预算法

C. 人均预算法

D. 比较预算法

58. 一般情况下，从学习成果、学习环境、（　　　）、培训成本等对培训方法进行比较和选择。

A. 培训目标

B. 培训内容

C. 培训组织

D. 培训成果转化

59. 对内部培训师的培训应集中在（　　）方面。

A. 公司战略

B. 培训技能

C. 组织文化

D. 核心价值观

60. 问卷调查法是以（　　）问卷形式设计一系列的问题，要求调查对象就问题进行打分或是非选择的方法。

A. 形式化

B. 标准化

C. 非形式化

D. 非标准化

三、多项选择题（下列每题的选项中，至少有 2 个是正确的）

1. 培训需求分析可以从（　　）等层面进行分析。

A. 组织层面

B. 任务层面

C. 战略层面

D. 人员层面

2. 组织分析包括（　　）等内容。

A. 明确组织战略导向

B. 了解组织人员结构

C. 了解组织氛围

D. 了解组织资源

3. 培训需求分析是指在需求调查的基础上，由（　　）等采取各种方法与技术，对组织内部各部门及其成员的目标绩效与能力结构及现有绩效和能力结构等进行比较分析。

A. 公司分管领导

B. 部门主管领导

C. 员工个人

D. 培训主管部门

E. 外部专家

4. 培训目标一般包括（　　）构成要素。

A. 内容要素

B. 技能要素

C. 条件要素

D. 标准要素

5. 培训目标所指向或预期的培训成果可分为（　　）。

A. 认知成果

B. 技能成果

C. 感情成果

D. 绩效成果和投资回报率

6. 确定培训目标的意义包括（　　）。

A. 培训活动效果评估的主要依据

B. 确定培训内容与培训方法的基本依据

C. 有利于引导受训者集中精力完成培训学习的任务

D. 有利于企业实现成本控制

7. 在编制培训预算时应遵循（　　）。

A. 合作原则

B. 准确性原则

C. 最优化原则

D. 速度原则

E. 普遍性原则

8. 培训需求分析的最佳时机包括（　　）。

A. 行业或相似组织中已经出现或经常出现的问题

B. 新设备或新程序引进时

C. 员工提升和晋级时

D. 利润上升和有充足的预算

9. 任务分析主要包括查看（　　），确定某个工作的业绩产出标准。

A. 工作评价

B. 工作描述

C. 访谈记录

D. 工作记录表

E. 工作规范

10. 培训目标的内容要素包括（　　）。

A. 知识的传授

B. 技能的培养

C. 性格的养成

D. 态度的转变

11. 下面哪几种培训师最好不要邀请来授课（　　　）。

A. 演讲型培训师

B. 讲师型培训师

C. 敏感型培训师

D. 专业型培训师

E. 弱型培训师

12. 培训的组织实施需要考虑的因素包括（　　　）。

A. 培训方法的选择

B. 培训师的选择

C. 培训机构的选择

D. 培训预算

13. 评价培训师的维度包括（　　　）。

A. 知识和经验

B. 与学员搞好关系

C. 个人魅力

D. 培训技能

14. 新技术培训的优越性在于（　　　）。

A. 培训时间灵活

B. 可随时接受培训

C. 适合各类培训课程

D. 降低异地培训的成本

E. 节省了管理费用

15. 访谈对象可以是（　　　）。

A. 组织的高层管理人员

B. 有关部门的负责人

C. 某些特殊岗位上的员工

D. 人力资源经理

16. 长期培训计划的重要性在于明确培训的（　　　）。

A. 方向性

B. 目标与现实之间的差距

C. 专业的配置

D. 受训者与培训内容的相关性

E. 受训者对培训项目的认知程度

17. 聘用外部培训师可能出现的问题（　　　）。

A. 兼职培训师对其日常工作的影响

B. 培训师对组织不熟悉

C. 组织对培训师不了解

D. 培训工作中的沟通和协调相对比较困难

18. 优秀培训师应该具备（　　　）。

A. 引导与应变能力

B. 策划与组织能力

C. 观察与捕捉能力

D. 分析和总结能力

19. 培训师需要具有（　　　）等特点。

A. 培训的热情

B. 有教学愿望

C. 来自受训者的尊敬

D. 耐心

20. （　　　）是培训预算的工作要点。

A. 统计培训对象信息

B. 培训预算的分配

C. 标准培训制度

D. 确定内外训比例

第四篇
绩效管理

本篇重点内容：

1. 绩效计划的制订原则、流程

2. 绩效指标设计原则、流程

3. 绩效评估方法及特点

4. 绩效反馈原则、流程

5. 绩效结果应用

绩效管理流程：

1. 制订绩效计划

2. 绩效实施与管理

3. 绩效评估

4. 绩效反馈与改进

5. 评估结果的应用

一、判断题（下列判断正确的请打"√"，错误的打"×"）

1. 绩效计划的制订必须与组织和部门的总体目标一致。

（　　）

2. 员工参与是绩效计划制订的重要形式。

（　　）

3. 绩效计划最终落实为订立正式书面协议即绩效计划和评估表，它是双方在明晰责、权、利的基础上签订的一个内部协议。

（　　）

4. 员工个人信息的准备工作包括员工所在岗位的工作描述和员工个人的绩效表现及评估结果。

（　　）

5. 绩效目标是指在特定时间内，按数量或质量标准对需要实现的结果所进行的陈述。

（　　）

6. 绩效目标应该来源于企业战略，从企业的最高层开始层层分解绩效目标。

（　　）

7. 绩效目标主要分为组织目标、部门目标、个人目标三个层次。

（　　）

8. 个人目标由主管下达，有利于企业绩效目标的执行效果。

（　　）

9. 在绩效目标分解中，可控目标是人员通过努力，只能影响其中的一部分，而无法全部实现，需由多个部门或多位人员承担。

（　　）

10. 在绩效目标分解中，可以把企业目标分为可控目标和可影响目标。

（　　）

11. 制订绩效计划时，需要遵循目标导向原则，即以目标为标准，随着目标的变化适时地调整和变更计划，使绩效计划能适应不断变化中的目标要求。

（　　）

12. 部门可影响目标是部门可以直接控制的目标，是该部门的关键目标。

（　　）

13. 确定绩效目标的原则是 SMART 原则，即指标必须是具体的，可衡量的，可达到的，高度相关的，以及具有时限性的。

（　　）

14. 绩效目标必须与企业和部门的目标高度相关，它是层层分解、自下而上的，具有明显的导向性。

（　　）

15. 目标管理法是一种潜在有效的评价员工绩效的方法，此方法普遍地运用于对专业人员和主管的评价上。

（　　）

16. 关键人员流失率目标，属于部门可控目标。

（　　）

17. 由于目标管理的时效性很强，所以它倾向于聚焦长期目标。

（　　）

18. 绩效目标制订之后，必须用书面确定下来，不能更改 。

（　　）

19. 行为锚定等级评价法的重点同时落在绩效结果和工作中表现出来的职

能性行为上。

（　　）

20. 行为锚定等级评价法一般是由主管和员工共同制定的。

（　　）

21. 目标管理法的一个主要缺点是设计需要很多时间和工作，而且需要为不同的工作制订不同的表格。

（　　）

22. 360度评估法因为实施和组织成本较大，因此一般是每半年一次。

（　　）

23. 绩效面谈是将员工的绩效表现通过非正式的渠道反馈给员工，以达到改善绩效的目的。

（　　）

24. 绩效评估指标的硬指标主要是指通过财务数据进行量化的指标。

（　　）

25. 绩效评估可以定期进行，也可以不定期进行。

（　　）

26. 为避免造成矛盾，进行反馈时，对错误行为的反馈应避免正面批评来进行。

（　　）

27. 360度评估法中，来自上级、下属、同事、客户的评估都可能出现偏差。

（　　）

28. 在将考评结果反馈给被考评者时，要允许员工对既定考评结果持有异议，同时更要同员工一道完成下一步改进的计划。

（　　）

29. 绩效面谈是指管理者要对员工的绩效表现进行打分，确定员工本周期的绩效表现，然后根据结果，与员工做一对一、面对面地进行沟通。

（　　）

30. 管理绩效也称关系绩效，是指员工通过额外的努力而准时完成某项任务时的表现。

（　　）

31. 360 度评估法适用于基层员工的考评。

（　　）

32. 关键事件法就是常说的 KPI。

（　　）

33. 关键事件法一般只能用作其他绩效评估方法的一种补充。

（　　）

34. 绩效面谈在员工绩效不佳时进行。

（　　）

35. 当这样一种行为对部门的效益产生无论是积极还是消极的重大影响时，主管都应把它记录下来，这样的事件便称为关键事件。

（　　）

36. 行为锚定法所依据的是员工在整个年度中的表现，而不是员工在最近一段时间的表现。

（　　）

37. "一个和尚挑水喝，两个和尚抬水喝，三个和尚没水喝"的现象，反映出来的是社会性"懈怠"。

（　　）

38. 绩效评估的结果可以用于个人在绩效改进、职业生涯发展方面提供借鉴。

（　　）

39. 绩效反馈时，强调个体的表现和贡献，而不是集体荣誉，是一种不当方式。

( )

40. 绩效面谈关注的重点是未来绩效的提高，而不是针对过去工作结果的奖惩。

( )

41. "批评"主要有两种方法，即"笨蛋效应"和 BEST 反馈。

( )

42. BEST 反馈的是一种对正确行为的反馈。

( )

43. 被评价人可以通过书面形式、电子邮件、口头汇报等形式提起绩效申诉。

( )

44. 在应用绩效评估结果时，应坚持以人为本，改进和提升员工的能力，促进员工的职业发展。

( )

45. 考评结果应告知员工，同时鼓励员工询问、质疑评估结果。

( )

46. 绩效面谈不需要事先通知员工。

( )

47. "SMART"原则是用来衡量绩效目标的有效性的，其中"R"指绩效目标是具有明显的导向性。

( )

48. 绩效面谈一般会占用较长时间，所以主管需要提前安排好被评估者的工作。

( )

49. 缺乏绩效申诉机制可能导致绩效评估前功尽弃。

（　　）

50. 使用关键事件法进行考察时，所依据的是员工在最近一段时间内的表现，而不是在整个年度中的表现。

（　　）

51. 绩效反馈是指确认工作绩效的不足和差距，查明产生的原因，制订并实施有针对性的改进计划和策略，不断提高竞争优势的过程。

（　　）

52. 处理完评价申诉后，应及时把令申诉者信服的处理结果告诉员工。

（　　）

53. 受理绩效投诉后，原评价流程暂时中断，但在投诉期间不影响薪酬的调整。

（　　）

54. 在处理绩效评估投诉时，要把处理评估申诉过程作为互动互进的过程，而不要简单地认为员工申诉"是员工有问题"。

（　　）

55. 绩效面谈是主管人员和员工之间一个双向交流、沟通的过程。

（　　）

56. 正向激励策略与负向激励策略是改进工作绩效的策略。

（　　）

57. 员工绩效评估结果申诉流程，涉及员工、人力资源部、高层管理者。

（　　）

58. 绩效评估结果应用范围主要包括制订绩效改进计划、薪酬奖金分配、正确处理内部员工关系等。

（　　）

59. 绩效评估结果是对员工进行职务调整的重要依据。

（　　）

60. 内部条件和外部环境都是影响绩效的主要因素，它们都是客观因素。

（　　）

二、单项选择题（下列每题的选项中，只有 1 个是正确的）

1. 绩效目标需要用（　　）组成这样一个格式来表示。

A. 绩效目标 + 计划值

B. 绩效目标 + 评估值

C. 绩效标准 + 指标值

D. 绩效标准 + 目标值

2. 当（　　）行为在特定环境中重复发生或仅发生一次，就会使管理者怀疑员工的个人能力。

A. 有效

B. 无效

C. 正式

D. 非正式

3. 在绩效计划的准备阶段，组织信息的准备，主要是对（　　）进行重温和再提高、再认识。

A. 个人目标

B. 团队目标

C. 部门目标

D. 组织目标

4. 在绩效计划的准备阶段，需要准备组织信息、部门信息和（　　　）。

A. 企业战略信息

B. 经营目标信息

C. 员工个人信息

D. 考核信息

5. （　　　）的评估与反馈是一个双向反馈过程。

A. 图表等级法

B. 360 度评估法

C. 关键事件法

D. 强制分布法

6. 目标管理法普遍运用于对（　　　）的评价上。

A. 专业人员和主管

B. 基层员工

C. 高层管理人员

D. 高级技术人员

7. 使用（　　　）进行考察时，所依据的是员工在最近一段时间内的表现，而不是在整个年度中的表现。

A. 目标管理法

B. 360 度评估法

C. 关键事件法

D. 行为锚定法

8. 绩效包括个人绩效和（　　　）两方面。

A. 工作绩效

B. 组织绩效

C. 关键绩效

D. 改进绩效

9. （　　）可以对被评估者进行全方位、多维度的绩效评估。

A. 图表等级法

B. 360 度评估法

C. 关键事件法

D. 强制分布法

10. 在绩效计划审定和确认阶段，直线经理与（　　）必须就绩效计划的主要内容进行再次的讨论和确定，保证双方能就内容所规定的各个方面达成共识。

A. 组织高层管理者

B. 人力资源部

C. 员工

D. 相关部门经理

11. 在确定绩效目标时，必须按（　　）流程进行。

①准备

②了解

③承诺

④讨论

⑤认可

A. ①—②—③—④—⑤

B. ④—①—③—②—⑤

C. ⑤—③—④—②—①

D. ②—①—④—③—⑤

12. 人员流失率目标、质量目标、降低管理成本等属于部门（　　）目标。

A. 可控

B. 可影响

C. 横向

D. 纵向

13. （ ）反映了目标管理法的优点。

A. 为主管向下属人员解释绩效评估结果提供了一些确切的事实证据

B. 符合绩效管理的目的

C. 可以强化客户中心的概念

D. 可以为某一员工的工作绩效提供具体反馈

14. 绩效目标应该来源于（ ），从企业的最高层开始层层分解绩效目标。

A. 部门目标

B. 绩效指标

C. 绩效计划

D. 企业战略

15. 绩效目标的设计要符合"SMART"原则，其中"S"意为（ ）。

A. 具体的

B. 背景

C. 技巧

D. 经验

16. 绩效计划最终落实为订立正式书面协议即（ ）。

A. 绩效目标和评估表

B. 绩效计划和评估表

C. 绩效计划和反馈表

D. 绩效目标和反馈表

17. （　　）不是绩效评估结果反馈的意义。

A. 评估公正的基础

B. 传递组织期望的手段

C. 工作目标和标准的契约

D. 绩效改进的前提

18. （　　）不是衡量绩效目标的要素。

A. 多用表现力较强的形容词

B. 保证目标明确具体

C. 有明确的衡量标准

D. 必须是合理有效的

19. 员工个人的绩效目标的来源包括组织的绩效目标、岗位职责和（　　）。

A. 内外部客户的需求

B. 绩效计划的要求

C. 部门的绩效目标

D. 个人职业发展需求

20. 绩效计划是由管理者与员工通过沟通协商共同制定的绩效目标、评估指标和（　　）的过程。

A. 绩效反馈

B. 实现绩效实施方案

C. 有效沟通

D. 绩效考评方法

21. 通过（　　），可以提升员工技能，从而提升绩效水平。

A. 招聘能力更高的员工

B. 技术开发

C. 加强培训

D. 加大激励力度

22. 主管人员在进行绩效面谈时，应当避免使用（ ）的语言，避免员工受到打击。

A. 中性化

B. 主观化

C. 客观化

D. 极端化

23. 以下不属于绩效考评原则的是（ ）。

A. 目标导向原则

B. 制度化原则

C. 全员参与原则

D. 可行性原则

24. 与员工一起沟通，设计绩效考评的指标和绩效目标的应该是（ ）。

A. 直接主管

B. 人力资源部

C. 被考评者

D. 绩效考评管理委员会

25. 绩效指标在设计中要避免主观臆断，始终牢记"针对岗位而非针对个人"标准，指标的选取要符合客观实际情况，以（ ）为依据。

A. 岗位职责

B. 绩效目标

C. 绩效计划

D. 部门目标

26. 平衡积分卡属于（ ）类型的实施办法。

A. 相对评价法

B. 绝对评价法

C. 描述法

D. 预测法

27. （　　）是部门或人员通过努力可以直接实现的。

A. 企业目标

B. 可控目标

C. 部门目标

D. 可影响目标

28. （　　）在设计中要避免主观臆断，始终牢记"针对岗位而非针对个人标准"。

A. 绩效目标

B. 部门目标

C. 绩效标准

D. 绩效指标

29. 绩效指标的提取通常采用头脑风暴法、问卷调查法、访谈法和（　　）等方法提取指标。

A. 资料档案收集法

B. 穷举法

C. 观察法

D. 自我评估法

30. 绩效计划的制订必须与组织和部门的总体目标一致是绩效计划的（　　）。

A. 全员参与原则

B. 可行性原则

C. 目标导向原则

D. 流程系统化原则

31. 强制分布法属于（　　）类型的实施办法。

A. 相对评价法

B. 绝对评价法

C. 描述法

D. 预测法

32. 全视角评估法（360 度评估法）属于（　　）类型的实施办法。

A. 相对评价法

B. 绝对评价法

C. 描述法

D. 预测法

33. 一个成功的绩效面谈需要事前精心准备，由主管人员和（　　）共同完成。

A. 人力资源经理

B. 员工

C. 人力资源部绩效主管

D. 部门经理

34. 以具体描述的特定工作行为是否被体现为基础来确定员工绩效水平的绩效评估方法，是绩效评估方法中的（　　）。

A. 关键绩效指标法

B. 行为锚定法

C. 描述法

D. 关键事件法

35. 通过（　　）把员工与组织发展有效地结合在一起。

A. 绩效计划

B. 绩效管理

C. 绩效实施

D. 绩效评估

36. 360 度评估法包括上级评估、下属评估、同事评估、自我评估和( )。

A. 问卷评估

B. 观察评估

C. 客户评估

D. 关键事件评估

37. ( ) 可以对被评估者的工作行为、个体特征做出比较全面的判断。

A. 关键事件法

B. 行为锚定法

C. 目标管理法

D. 360 度评估法

38. 绩效考评的内容可分 ( ) 三类。

A. 态度指标、业绩指标、能力指标

B. 行为指标、结果指标、素质指标

C. 态度指标、绩效指标、结果指标

D. 行为指标、绩效指标、能力指标

39. 如果要采用既操作简单开发成本又较低的考评方法，可采用( )。

A. 目标管理法

B. 360 度评估法

C. 关键绩效指标法

D. 行为锚定法

40. 360 度评估法的适用人群范围是（　　）。

A. 所有员工

B. 中高层管理者

C. 技术人员

D. 营销人员

41. "一个和尚挑水喝，两个和尚抬水喝，三个和尚没水喝。"是（　　）现象。

A. 社会性懈怠

B. 汉堡原理

C. 晕轮效应

D. 暗示

42. 360 度评估工具一般采用（　　）。

A. 问卷调查法

B. 访谈法

C. 抽样调查法

D. 相对评估法

43. 当一种行为对部门的效益产生的是（　　）重大影响时，这样的行为被称为关键事件。

A. 消极的

B. 主动的

C. 正面的

D. 严重的

44. 在运用关键事件法进行评估时，在每（　　）左右的时间里，主管和其下属见一次面。

A. 3 个月

B. 6 个月

C. 9 个月

D. 12 个月

45. 绩效评估前需要进行评估培训，培训对象包括管理人员和（   ）。

A. 企业中高层管理者

B. 员工

C. 人力资源部工作人员

D. 需要参与评估的客户

46. （   ）不是绩效计划实施的相关主体。

A. 人力资源专业人员

B. 人力资源委员会

C. 员工

D. 管理者

47. （   ）不是目标管理法的优点。

A. 符合绩效管理的目的

B. 成本较大

C. 比较公平

D. 增加了员工的自主性

48. 在绩效评估结果评定时，由（   ）发放绩效评估表。

A. 部门经理

B. 团队主管

C. 人力资源部

D. 直线经理

49. 获得（　　）的支持是 360 度评估实施的前提。

A. 评估小组

B. 人力资源部主管

C. 高层领导

D. 部门主管

50. （　　）作为人力资源管理的程序，评估结果应有利于人力资源的管理和决策。

A. 绩效投诉

B. 绩效评估

C. 绩效反馈

D. 绩效面谈

51. 在绩效反馈时，先对被评估者表现积极的地方表扬，再对其需要改进的工作进行批评指正，最后以肯定和支持结束，是（　　）的沟通技巧。

A. 胡萝卜加大棒

B. 汉堡原理

C. BEST 反馈

D. 笨蛋效应

52. 绩效评估结果的反馈应以（　　）为重点。

A. 奖励

B. 惩罚

C. 辅导

D. 激励

53. 同一层级、同一职务及同一性质岗位的指标在横向上必须保持一致，便于绩效考核时分出不同等级，是绩效指标设计的（　　）原则。

A. 可操作性

B. 界限清楚

C. 客观公正

D. 可比性

54. （　　）反馈以教与问相结合为特点，评估者对被评估者所反馈的内容更感兴趣。

A. 指令式

B. 授权式

C. 交谈式

D. 指导式

55. （　　）不是行为锚定法的优点。

A. 设计需要相当多的时间和工作

B. 由实际完成工作的员工根据其观察和经验制定出来

C. 其评价可以为某一员工的工作绩效提供具体反馈

D. 其制定过程增加了该方法被接受的可能性

56. 在绩效反馈面谈之后，被评价人对自己的评价成绩有异议的，可以向（　　）进行投诉。

A. 主管

B. 人力资源部

C. 主管的上级或人力资源部门

D. 公司领导

57. （　　）应作为独立的第三方分别与评估人和被评估人面谈，协商并寻求解决纠纷的方法。

A. 人力资源部

B. 主管的上级

C. 职工代表

D. 公司分管领导

58. 接受绩效申诉以后，查证工作应在（　　）完成。

A. 1 周内

B. 2 周内

C. 3 周内

D. 1 个月内

59. 绩效评估结果的应用与（　　）紧密结合。

A. 员工利益

B. 主管绩效

C. 部门利益

D. 公司利益

60. （　　）不是绩效改进过程中分析工作绩效差距的方法。

A. 水平比较法

B. 目标比较法

C. 横向比较法

D. 纵向比较法

三、多项选择题（下列每题的选项中，至少有 2 个是正确的）

1. 绩效目标主要分为组织目标、部门目标、个人目标三个层次，根据绩效目标的三个层次，负责绩效目标制定的责任人应该是（　　）。

A. 公司决策层

B. 人力资源部

C. 部门领导

D. 个人

2. 在评估周期的选择上，一般要注意（　　）几个方面。

A. 评估时间的选择，应注意避开员工的工作高峰

B. 一定要采取不定期的评估

C. 不同层次企业人员，评估周期不一

D. 在评估期内，员工应该已经完成了他们的工作

3. 根据360度评估法的定义及被评估者的信息来源，360度评估法的考评人员应该是凡是与被考评者有工作关系的都应当参与到考评当中，即（　　）。

A. 被评估者的同事

B. 被评估者的服务对象

C. 被评估者的上级

D. 被评估者的下属

4. 绩效指标在设计过程中需要遵循（　　）原则。

A. 客观公正性

B. 数量少而精

C. 界限清楚

D. 明确具体性

5. 绩效计划实施的相关主体包括（　　）以及员工个人。

A. 管理者

B. 组织人力资源专业人员

C. 各团队

D. 各部门

6. 绩效面谈的计划主要是对（　　）做出相应的安排。

A. 面谈内容

B. 面谈地点

C. 面谈人员

D. 面谈时间

7. 应用绩效结果时需要防范哪些问题（　　　）。

A. 没有及时反馈给被评估者

B. 没有应用到与员工利益紧密结合的地方

C. 没有针对员工需要培训和改进的地方

D. 应用方式单一，形式化严重

8. 在绩效目标的设定过程中，员工个人的绩效目标来源于（　　　）。

A. 岗位职责

B. 战略目标

C. 内外部客户的需求

D. 组织的绩效目标

9. 在绩效改进过程中，分析工作绩效差距的方法有（　　　）。

A. 横向比较法

B. 目标比较法

C. 水平比较法

D. 外部比较法

10. 绩效指标通常包括（　　　）等要素。

A. 标度

B. 标志

C. 指标名称

D. 指标定义

11. 影响绩效的主要因素有（　　　）。

A. 外部环境

B. 激励效应

C. 内部条件

D. 员工技能

12. 处理绩效评估投诉应注意的事项有（　　）。

A. 具体分析投诉内容

B. 找出问题发生的原因

C. 处理评价申诉，应当把令申诉者信服的处理结果告诉员工

D. 要把处理评价申诉过程作为互动互进的过程

13. 绩效评估结果应用的范围有（　　）。

A. 薪酬奖金的分配

B. 提供有针对性的培训

C. 进行员工职业生涯规划

D. 进行职务调整

14. 员工对绩效评估的结果有异议时，可以提出申诉，人力资源部受理申诉后，必须分不同场合向（　　）了解情况，以确保所了解的信息真实客观。

A. 评估人

B. 被评估人

C. 人力资源部经理

D. 评估人的上级领导

15. 通过对管理人员的绩效评估培训，可以（　　）。

A. 提高员工的技能

B. 学习如何避免在评估中出现的人为误差

C. 掌握绩效评估中需要用到的一些技术和方法

D. 加强他们对绩效评估的认识

16. 按绩效评估的角度分，可将绩效指标分为（　　）。

A. 周边绩效

B. 业绩指标

C. 管理绩效

D. 任务绩效

17. 行为锚定等级评价法一般是由主管和员工共同参加一系列会议后制定出来，它通常有（　　）步骤。

A. 主管与有关员工为每个工作维度编写出尽可能多的行为锚定

B. 主管与工作承担者对所采用的分值及每一分值的锚定叙述分类达成一致意见

C. 主管与有关员工自上而下进行总目标的分解和责任落实

D. 主管与有关员工确定工作的相关维度

18. 绩效计划制订的流程是（　　）。

A. 准备阶段

B. 沟通阶段

C. 审定和确认阶段

D. 实施阶段

19. 绩效评估申诉的流程包括提出申诉、（　　）等。

A. 投诉受理

B. 查证工作

C. 召开投诉处理会议

D. 评估成绩调整

20. 绩效评估结果应用的原则是（　　）。

A. 评估结果应及时反馈给被评估者

B. 绩效评估作为人力资源管理的程度，评估结果应有利于人力资源的管理和决策

C. 坚持以人为本，改进和提升职工的绩效，促进员工的职业发展

D. 能够将员工个人的利益与组织群体的利益紧密联系起来，使员工和组织共荣辱、共成长

第五篇

薪酬与福利管理

本篇重点内容：

1. 薪酬管理原则

2. 岗位评价原则、方法和流程

3. 薪酬调查渠道和流程

4. 薪酬结构设计原则、流程

5. 薪酬水平策略选择

6. 宽带薪酬设计步骤和注意事项

薪酬与福利管理流程：

1. 确定薪酬原则和策略

2. 工作分析和岗位评价

3. 薪酬市场调查

4. 薪酬水平确定

5. 薪酬结构设计

6. 实施与修正

一、判断题（下列判断正确的请打"√"，错误的打"×"）

1. 薪酬是企业对员工给企业所做的贡献的相应回报。

（　　）

2. 岗位评价主要是用于设计薪酬结构和评价任职员工的绩效。

（　　）

3. 岗位评价又称职位评估或工作评价，是按照一定的客观衡量标准，采用一定的方法，对岗位的性质、难易程度、劳动强度、责任大小、任职资格等进行评价的过程。

（　　）

4. 岗位评价的目的是衡量企业内部每一岗位的价值，并建立各岗位价值间的相对关系。岗位评价的主要依据是工作分析的信息。

（　　）

5. 通过岗位评价，明确了岗位之间的相对价值大小，从而可以为岗位分级等。

（　　）

6. 基准岗位的特征之一是这些岗位上有相当数量的劳动力被雇佣。

（　　）

7. 让员工积极地参与到岗位评估工作中来，容易让他们对岗位评估的结果产生认同。

（　　）

8. 选择薪酬调查的岗位通常是基准岗位。

（　　）

9. 排序法的优点在于快速、简单、费用比较低，而且容易和员工进行沟通。

（　　）

10. 要素计点法的缺点在于容易受他人的主观影响。

（　　）

11. 要素计点法是指把岗位按照一系列事先确定好的等级进行分组和归类。

（　　）

12. 一般而言，岗位调查的对象仅包括基准岗位。

（　　）

13. 岗位评价的结果确定了岗位之间的相对价值，从而解决了薪酬水平的问题。

（　　）

14. 要素比较法是一种精确、量化和系统的方法，其每一步操作都有详细、可靠的说明，可靠性比较高、减少主观性，但实践中不常用。

（　　）

15. 基准岗位确定是薪酬调查的第二个步骤。基准岗位必须是组织内独有的岗位 。

（　　）

16. 薪幅 =（薪酬最大值 + 薪酬最小值）/2。

（　　）

17. 企业的薪酬政策线是为了确保内部薪酬符合国家的相关规定。

（　　）

18. 内部薪酬调查是针对企业内部薪酬设计的历史演变情况的调查。

（　　）

19. 企业整体薪酬水平高并不意味着薪酬的外部竞争力大。

（   ）

20. 外部薪酬调查是针对企业外部、本行业内的薪酬状况进行的调查。

（   ）

21. 岗位评价应组织专门人员进行，其中不应当包括在其岗位上工作的人员，以确保客观性。

（   ）

22. 薪酬调查的内容包括长期财务性薪酬和短期财务性薪酬。

（   ）

23. 海氏评价法有效地解决了不同部门的不同职务之间相对价值的相互比较和量化的难题。

（   ）

24. 分红甚至股份作为薪酬结构的一个环节，主要适用于中低层管理人员。

（   ）

25. 企业在高速增长阶段，应选择薪酬水平跟随策略。

（   ）

26. 某企业对于其核心与关键性岗位采用了市场领先薪酬策略，而对于普通岗位则采用市场跟随策略，这一策略称为成本导向策略。

（   ）

27. 企业总是在追求利润最大化，而控制总成本是实现利润最大化的有效途径。

（   ）

28. 薪酬策略是企业薪酬政策与管理价值观的集中体现。

（   ）

29. 薪酬调查要尽可能多地覆盖企业内的岗位。

（　　）

30. 薪酬调查的基准岗位必须满足两个条件，是组织内具有代表性的岗位，同时也是行业内普遍存在的通用岗位。

（　　）

31. 从应聘人员那里获得相关企业的薪酬信息是一种不道德的薪酬调查渠道。

（　　）

32. 薪酬的激励性原则，指薪酬结构与组织层次、职位设计之间形成的对等、协调关系。

（　　）

33. 政府人才交流部门定期发布的岗位薪酬参考信息，由于覆盖面广、薪酬范围大，对有些企业没有意义。

（　　）

34. 工作任务和流程强调团队合作时，团队成员间薪酬应尽量拉大差距。

（　　）

35. 薪酬水平是指企业支付给不同职位的平均薪酬。

（　　）

36. 企业要留住人才，只要提供具有竞争力的工资就可以了。

（　　）

37. 控制劳动力成本，是企业薪酬外部竞争力的体现。

（　　）

38. 企业建立薪酬制度时"对外相对公平，对内有竞争力"的要求在现实操作中经常产生矛盾。

（　　）

39. 《工资集体协商试行办法》主要是对企业的约束力。

（　　）

40. 岗位稀缺性、集体工资协议等都是制约薪酬水平的因素。

（　　）

41. 通过薪酬结构合理设计，达成企业内部各个岗位之间的相对公平，可确保企业合理控制成本，帮助企业有效激励员工。

（　　）

42. 宽带薪酬在坚持以岗定酬的同时，考虑个人能力、资历的差别因素，因此更注重内部公平。

（　　）

43. 对外竞争力、对内公平性是薪酬体系设计的基本原则。

（　　）

44. 对外竞争力是指薪酬结构与组织层次、职位设计之间形成的对等、协调关系。

（　　）

45. 一个好的薪酬体系可以不必随着企业战略的改变而改变。

（　　）

46. 生产线上的工人宜采用一岗多薪制。

（　　）

47. 汽车制造业是高科技企业，适合宽带薪酬。

（　　）

48. 受企业外部环境和内部条件变化的影响，不同职位或技能对创造企业价值的贡献会发生相应的变化。因此，需要定期诊断和调整企业的薪酬结构，是薪酬结构设计与组织结构一致的原则。

（　　）

49. 弹性薪酬模式适合于初创期的企业。

（　　）

50. 折中薪酬模式原理合适，但科学合理设计的难度很大。

（　　）

51. 薪酬主要取决于工龄与企业的经营状况，与个人的绩效关联不大，员工收入相对稳定，是折中薪酬模式。

（　　）

52. 宽带薪酬也称海氏薪酬制。其实质就是从原来注重岗位薪酬转变为注重绩效薪酬。

（　　）

53. "扁平化"组织结构宜采用一岗多薪制。

（　　）

54. 工资分级就是把多种类型工作对应的工资值合并组合成若干等级，形成一个工资等级系列。

（　　）

55. 职等是指将不同职系中，工作难易繁简程度、工作责任大小、上岗资格条件等相同相似的职级，纳入统一档次，使各个职级之间打破职系的界限产生纵向的平衡关系。

（　　）

56. 一岗一薪制的另一个缺点是不能进行薪酬调整，尤其是薪酬的个体调整问题。

（　　）

57. 一岗多薪制下，员工工资等级的晋升不以岗位晋升为前提。

（　　）

58. 稳定薪酬模式的优点是员工主动性强、积极性高。 （ ）

59. 岗位排序法是一种非量化的简单的岗位评价方法。

（ ）

60. 宽带薪酬的实质就是从原来注重岗位薪酬转变为注重绩效薪酬。

（ ）

二、单项选择题（下列每题的选项中，只有 1 个是正确的）

1. 对于大多数劳动者而言，（ ）是保证其日常生活正常进行的经济基础。

A. 薪酬

B. 奖金

C. 福利

D. 津贴

2. 岗位评价的结果确定了岗位之间的相对价值，从而解决了（ ）问题。

A. 对员工的激励性

B. 合法性和经济性

C. 内部公平性

D. 外部竞争性

3. 制定薪酬的原则不包括（ ）。

A. 对员工的激励性

B. 弹性

C. 内部公平性

D. 外部竞争性

4. 一般多用于部门内岗位评估的方法是（　　）。

A. 排序法

B. 分类套级法

C. 要素比较法

D. 要素计点法

5. 选择薪酬调查的岗位通常使用（　　）岗位确定法。

A. 管理

B. 普通

C. 技术

D. 基准

6. 排序法一般不适用于岗位数量超过（　　）个的情况。

A. 10

B. 15

C. 20

D. 25

7. （　　）企业不适合宽带薪酬。

A. 外资型

B. 技术型

C. 创新型

D. 劳动密集型

8. （　　）属于量化的岗位评估方法。

A. 排序法

B. 分类套级法

C. 要素比较法

D. 要素计点法

9. (   ) 不是企业薪酬设计要满足的要求。

A. 外部竞争性

B. 内部公平性

C. 合法性

D. 可控性

10. 薪酬调查的步骤是 (   )。

A. 确定调查目的→确定基准岗位→确定调查的范围和对象→确定调查的内容和项目→选择调查方式→整理、修正和分析调查数据

B. 确定调查目的→确定调查的范围和对象→确定基准岗位→确定调查的内容和项目→选择调查方式→整理、修正和分析调查数据

C. 确定调查目的→确定调查的内容和项目→确定基准岗位→确定调查的范围和对象→选择调查方式→整理、修正和分析调查数据

D. 确定调查目的→选择调查方式→确定调查的范围和对象→确定调查的内容和项目→确定基准岗位→整理、修正和分析调查数据

11. 要素比较法需要选择 (   ) 个关键岗位。

A. 10

B. 10 ~ 15

C. 15 ~ 20

D. 25

12. 下面关于主要的薪酬调查渠道论述正确的是 (   )。

A. 企业之间的相互调查

B. 从公开的信息中了解

C. 从其他企业到本企业来的应聘人员也可以了解该企业的薪酬状况

D. 以上都是

13. 企业通常通过外部薪酬调查来解决 (   ) 问题。

A. 对员工的激励性

B. 合法性和经济性

C. 内部公平性

D. 外部竞争性

14. （   ）不是企业薪酬设计要满足的要求。

A. 外部竞争性

B. 内部公平性

C. 合法性

D. 可控性

15. （   ）也可称为权变策略。

A. 市场领先策略

B. 市场跟随策略

C. 成本导向策略

D. 混合薪酬策略

16. （   ）又称指导图表—形状构成法。

A. 要素计点法

B. 要素比较法

C. 岗位分类法

D. 岗位排列法

E. 海氏评价法

17. 岗位评价时，（   ）的优点是简单、容易解释、执行起来速度快、对评估者的培训要求少等。

A. 排序法

B. 分类套级法

C. 要素比较法

D. 要素计点法

18. （　　）岗位评价法有效地解决了不同职能部门的不同职务之间相对价值的相互比较和量化的难题，被企业界广泛接受。

A. 要素计点法

B. 要素比较法

C. 岗位分类法

D. 岗位排列法

19. （　　）岗位评价法广泛应用于蓝领和白领岗位。

A. 要素计点法

B. 要素比较法

C. 岗位分类法

D. 岗位排列法

20. （　　）不是薪酬调查的内容。

A. 组织信息

B. 薪酬要素信息

C. 岗位的总体薪酬结构和水平

D. 薪酬战略

21. 最常见的报酬要素是劳动技能、劳动责任、（　　）和劳动保护环境四类。

A. 劳动时间

B. 劳动强度

C. 劳动内容

D. 劳动效率

22. （　　）岗位评价法在实践中并不常用。

A. 要素计点法

B. 要素比较法

C. 岗位分类法

D. 岗位排列法

23. （　　）岗位评价法的特征是能够快速地对大量的岗位进行评价。

A. 要素计点法

B. 要素比较法

C. 分类套级法

D. 岗位排序法

24. （　　）岗位评价法更适用于同一个部门内部的岗位排列。

A. 要素计点法

B. 要素比较法

C. 分类套级法

D. 排序法

25. 实行的是成本导向战略，考虑尽可能地节约企业生产、经营和管理的成本，这种情况下一般采用（　　）的薪酬水平策略。

A. 市场领先

B. 市场跟随

C. 成本导向

D. 差异化薪酬

26. 关于企业薪酬管理原则，说法不正确的是（　　）。

A. 对员工有普遍性

B. 对外有竞争力

C. 对内公平

D. 经济性及合法性

27. 企业薪酬水平受其（　　）制约。

A. 支付能力

B. 企业性质

C. 企业规模

D. 薪酬制度

28. （　　）不是岗位评价的原则。

A. 岗位评价一定要有外部顾问

B. 对岗不对人

C. 让员工积极参与到岗位评价中

D. 岗位评价结果应该公开

29. 当企业处于再造阶段时，企业应及时调整薪酬水平策略，往往会采用
（　　）。

A. 市场领先策略

B. 市场跟随策略

C. 滞后策略

D. 差异化薪酬策略

30. 企业处于高速成长阶段应选择（　　）薪酬水平策略。

A. 市场跟随

B. 成本导向

C. 市场领先

D. 混合薪酬

31. （　　）不是薪酬水平的外部竞争力的体现方式。

A. 吸引、保留和激励员工

B. 增强企业的实力

C. 塑造企业形象

D. 工资水平提高

32. 薪酬结构设计可以用来检验已有的薪酬体系的（   ）。

A. 合理性

B. 等级性

C. 补偿性

D. 集体性

33. 薪酬中位值是3000，薪酬变动率是50%，那么薪酬最大值是（   ）。

A. 3200

B. 3600

C. 4000

D. 4500

34. 薪酬最大值是4500，最小值是3000，那么薪酬变动率是（   ）。

A. 33%

B. 50%

C. 170%

D. 250%

35. 薪酬最大值是4500，最小值是3000，那么薪酬中位值是（   ）。

A. 3000

B. 3250

C. 3500

D. 3750

36. 薪酬中位值是3000，薪酬变动率是50%，那么薪酬最小值是（   ）。

A. 2400

B. 3000

C. 3600

D. 4200

37. （   ）的员工流动率大。

A. 稳定薪酬模式

B. 弹性薪酬模式

C. 折中薪酬模式

D. 可变薪酬模式

38. （   ）的员工忠诚度高。

A. 稳定薪酬模式

B. 弹性薪酬模式

C. 折中薪酬模式

D. 可变薪酬模式

39. 在设计（   ）的薪酬时，要考虑分红甚至股份的设计。

A. 营销人员

B. 中层

C. 高管人员

D. 普通岗位

40. 一般情况下企业会采取（   ），即薪酬主要却取决于任职者岗位以及绩效状况，与团队、个人的绩效有一定关联，员工大部分收入相对稳定。

A. 稳定薪酬模式

B. 弹性薪酬模式

C. 折中薪酬模式

D. 可变薪酬模式

41. 薪酬结构调整的依据是（   ）和员工能力对企业贡献的大小。

A. 劳动强度

B. 岗位价值

C. 工作环境

D. 工作责任

42. （　　）是薪酬结构设计的流程。

A. 设计工资职等数目→确定薪酬最小值、最大值→设计工资职等中位值及确定职等薪酬增长率→设计薪酬幅度

B. 确定薪酬最小值、最大值→设计工资职等数目→设计薪酬幅度→设计工资职等中位值及确定职等薪酬增长率

C. 设计工资职等数目→设计薪酬幅度→确定薪酬最小值、最大值→设计工资职等中位值及确定职等薪酬增长率

D. 确定薪酬最小值、最大值→设计工资职等数目→设计工资职等中位值及确定职等薪酬增长率→设计薪酬幅度

43. 如果某企业内部各岗位差别很明显，那么最好采用（　　）进行岗位评价。

A. 岗位排序法

B. 岗位分类法

C. 要素比较法

D. 要素计点法

44. 标准化程度高、技术较为单一、工作结果产出统一、岗位比较稳定的岗位或企业，比如生产线上的工人等，适合（　　）。

A. 一岗一薪制

B. 一岗多薪制

C. 宽带薪酬制

D. 多岗一薪制

45. （　　）不是要素计点法的优点。

A. 提供精确的评价标准

B. 不易受人主观影响

C. 是一种较为详细的、分析性的方法

D. 执行起来速度快

46. 采取计件或提成工资制的企业，采用的是（　　）薪酬模式。

A. 混合

B. 稳定

C. 折中

D. 弹性

47. 某企业的发展战略是维持企业不至于倒闭，应选择（　　）策略。

A. 市场领先薪酬

B. 薪酬水平滞后

C. 高薪吸引人才

D. 拉大薪酬差距

48. （　　）薪酬模式是激励效应比较强的薪酬方式。

A. 稳定

B. 市场跟随

C. 弹性

D. 折中

49. （　　）更注重内部公平。

A. 一岗一薪制

B. 一岗多薪制

C. 工资分级

D. 工资分等

50. 若 A 公司为民营企业，刚刚起步不久，比较适用的薪酬模式是（　　）。

A. 稳定薪酬模式

B. 弹性薪酬模式

C. 折中薪酬模式

D. 侧重职位的薪酬模式

51. B 公司的发展战略为"保持利润与保护市场"，那它可采用的薪酬水平是（　　）。

A. 高于平均水平的薪酬

B. 平均水平的薪酬

C. 低于平均水平的薪酬

D. 远远低于平均水平的薪酬

52. C 公司采取的薪酬策略为着重成本控制，那么它可能处于（　　）阶段。

A. 合并

B. 迅速发展

C. 正常发展

D. 衰退

53. 下列哪项不是影响薪酬水平的因素（　　）。

A. 法律的规定

B. 高层领导的意见

C. 劳动力市场价格

D. 企业的支付能力

54. 在实践中，企业工资等级系列平均在（　　）。

A. 7~10 级

B. 10~15 级

C. 15~20 级

D. 20~25 级

55. 宽带薪酬中的"带"是指（　　）。

A. 薪酬幅度

B. 薪酬级别

C. 薪酬模式

D. 薪酬策略

56. 下面哪一项对宽带薪酬的描述是不正确的（　　　）。

A. 良好的绩效管理是宽带薪酬制度应用的基础

B. 技术型、创新型的企业尤为适合宽带薪酬

C. 成熟的管理队伍必不可少

D. 创业初期企业适合宽带薪酬

57. （　　　）是非量化的评估方法。

A. 海氏评价法

B. 排序法

C. 要素计点法

D. 要素比较法

58. （　　　）是排序法的操作步骤。

A. 获取岗位信息→选择报酬要素并对岗位进行分类→对岗位进行排序→综合排序结果

B. 选择报酬要素并对岗位进行分类→获取岗位信息→对岗位进行排序→综合排序结果

C. 选择报酬要素并对岗位进行分类→对岗位进行排序→获取岗位信息→综合排序结果

D. 获取岗位信息→对岗位进行排序→选择报酬要素并对岗位进行分类→综合排序结果

59. （　　　）企业适合使用宽带薪酬。

A. 创业期企业

B. 汽车厂

C. 知名外贸企业

D. 银行

60. 一种典型的宽带薪酬结构可能只有（　　）个职等。

A. 4～8

B. 8～10

C. 10～15

D. 15～20

三、多项选择题（下列每题的选项中，至少有 2 个是正确的）

1. 岗位评价的流程包括成立岗位评价小组（　　）。

A. 选择方法

B. 制定薪酬等级

C. 确定岗位等级

D. 进行工作分析

2. 排序法的缺点包括（　　）。

A. 在排序方面很难达成共识

B. 不能体现岗位之间的差异究竟有多大

C. 跨部门岗位之间排序比较困难

D. 岗位超过一定数量难度激增，跨部门岗位之间排序比较困难

3. 薪酬结构设计是薪酬体系的一个重要模块，应遵循（　　）原则。

A. 内部一致性

B. 动态调整性

C. 外部竞争性

D. 合法性

4. 岗位评价方法中，（   ）采用的都是报酬要素。

A. 排序法

B. 分类套级法

C. 要素比较法

D. 要素计点法

5. （   ）是岗位评价的原则。

A. 不相容职务分离

B. 对岗不对人

C. 员工参与

D. 评估结果公开

E. 体现公司的战略发展方向

6. 在实际操作中，最常见的报酬要素是（   ）。

A. 劳动技能

B. 劳动责任

C. 劳动时间

D. 劳动环境

E. 劳动强度

7. 在海氏评价法中，所有职务所包含的最主要的付酬要素包括（   ）。

A. 技能水平

B. 劳动环境

C. 解决问题的能力

D. 承担的职务责任

8. （   ）是制约薪酬水平的因素。

A. 法律的规定

B. 企业效益和支付能力

C. 劳动力市场价格

D. 工作岗位

E. 部门和个人绩效

9. （   ）是薪酬结构设计的目的。

A. 让人才脱颖而出

B. 吸引关键人才

C. 基本的安全保障

D. 岗位价值肯定

E. 员工与公司结成利益共同体

10. （   ）等是企业采用的降低工资水平的短期措施。

A. 延缓提薪

B. 工资冻结

C. 冻结福利项目

D. 暂停生活补贴

11. 关键性岗位的特点包括（   ）。

A. 对员工和组织是非常重要的

B. 工作要求大致相同

C. 有稳定的工作内容

D. 在薪酬调查中，可以对关键性岗位进行市场调查

12. 岗位评价的目的包括（   ）。

A. 确定职位级别

B. 确定岗位的绝对价值

C. 确定员工晋升资格的依据之一

D. 员工职业发展的参照

13. 薪酬调查的基准岗位通常具有（　　）等特征。

A. 岗位内容众所周知、相对稳定，且得到从事该岗位员工的广泛认可

B. 这些岗位的供求不平衡，市场供应过剩

C. 这些岗位能代表当前所研究的完整的岗位结构

D. 这些岗位上有相当数量的劳动力被雇佣

14. 外部薪酬调查是针对企业外部市场的薪酬状况进行的调查，实施中要考虑的因素包括（　　）。

A. 企业选择

B. 方法选择

C. 岗位选择

D. 内容选择

15. 薪酬调查中最重要的资料是支付给在职者的实际薪酬率，包括（　　）等。

A. 加薪周期

B. 工作日长短

C. 最后增资的日期和幅度

D. 红利及激励工资

16. 宽带薪酬的特征包括（　　）。

A. 薪酬等级层次少

B. 访谈法薪酬等级最高值与最低值之间的区间变动比率高

C. 宽带薪酬为员工提供更多的横向发展空间

D. 宽带薪酬适用于创业型企业

17. （　　）类型、条件的企业适宜宽带薪酬模式。

A. 劳动密集型企业

B. 技术型、创新型的高科技企业

C. 创业阶段

D. 人力资源管理体系健全

E. 企业管理队伍成熟

18.（　　）是企业可采取的薪酬水平策略。

A. 市场领先策略

B. 市场跟随策略

C. 成本导向策略

D. 混合薪酬策略

E. 紧缩策略

19.（　　）体现了薪酬水平的外部竞争力。

A. 解雇高级管理人员

B. 吸引、保留和激励员工

C. 控制劳动力成本

D. 增强企业实力

E. 塑造企业形象

20. 在进行薪酬调查时，要注意几点原则，包括（　　）等。

A. 要在被调查企业不知晓的情况下进行调研以获得真实数据

B. 调查的资料要准确

C. 调查的资料要随时更新

D. 要确定岗位职责与本企业的岗位职责完全相同

第六篇
劳动关系管理

本篇重点内容：

1. 员工关系管理的必要性

2. 员工手册编制

3. 劳动规章制度编制

4. 集体协商与集体合同

5. 职工代表大会性质

一、判断题（下列判断正确的请打"√"，错误的打"×"）

1. 员工关系是指员工与公司、员工与员工之间的关系，就是劳资关系的一个称谓。

（　　）

2. 员工关系管理其实就是企业与员工的沟通管理。

（　　）

3. 员工关系强调以员工为主体和出发点的企业内部关系，注重个体层次上的关系和交流，关注的是和谐与合作 。

（　　）

4. 劳动规章制度是员工关系管理的主要载体。

（　　）

5. 休息休假主要包括：日休息时间、周休息日安排、年休假办法、不能实际标准工时职工的休息虚假、其他假期。

（　　）

6. 和谐的员工关系是激励员工、减轻工作压力的重要手段之一。

（　　）

7. 劳动纪律是有效的管理工具、员工的行动指南。

（　　）

8. 劳动规章制度又称企业内部劳动规章、内部劳动准则，是指用人单位依法制定并在本单位内部实施的组织劳动和进行劳动管理的规则。

（　　）

9. 员工关系管理的主要职责是：协调员工与公司之间、员工与员工之间的关系，引导建立积极向上的工作环境。

（　　）

10. 企业制定的劳动规章制度调整范围仅仅限于与企业有劳动契约关系的特定劳动者，不能适用于其他不特定的人。

（　　）

11. 职工无权参与劳动规章制度的制定。

（　　）

12. 企业制定劳动规章制度，必须经过民主协商程序，兼顾企业与劳动者的合法权益才能具有法律效力。

（　　）

13. 企业规章制度是企业内部的事情，只要不违法，一般不要求将其制定的劳动规章制度报送劳动行政部门备案。

（　　）

14. 惩戒处分是指用人单位为保障自身生产经营活动的顺利进行对劳动者违反企业劳动规章制度的行为进行制裁。

（　　）

15. 劳动纪律是用人单位依法制定的、用人单位和全体职工在劳动过程中必须遵守的行为规则。

（　　）

16. 劳动纪律起草过程中应当征求工会、员工代表意见。

（　　）

17. 用人单位有权自主决定对模范职工进行奖励和对违纪者进行惩罚。

（　　）

18. 劳动纪律的内容一般应当包括时间纪律、组织纪律、岗位纪律、职场纪律等。

（　　）

19. 用人单位不得以随意解除劳动合同的方式惩戒职工。

（　　）

20. 集体协商的主体一是劳动者，二是用人单位。

（　　）

21. 集体协商主要采取协商会议的形式，是一种高度规范化、程序化的商谈。

（　　）

22. 集体协商时用人单位协商代表与职工协商代表可相互兼任。

（　　）

23. 劳动纪律规定的内容要在法律允许的范围和程度内对职工行为进行约束，不得违法限制和剥夺职工依法享有的权利和自由，对违纪职工不得采取法定限额外的惩罚措施，这是劳动纪律的公平平等原则。

（　　）

24. 所有的劳动合同均可以约定试用期。

（　　）

25. 制定劳动纪律和惩戒制度是企业依法享有的自主权，但其权利行使受企业规章制度的约束。

（　　）

26. 劳动纪律的公示方法包括：公布、培训、员工签字、企业发文、办公会议讨论、职代会通过、内部局域网发布、公证、刊登于内刊厂报等。

（　　）

27. 为了涵盖一些不能预见的情况，可在劳动纪律中加入"其他严重违反劳动纪律行为等"的条款。

（　　）

28. 签订集体合同产生争议、双方当事人不能协商解决的，当事人一方或双方可向企业劳动争议调解委员会提出协调处理的书面申请。

（　　）

29. 用人单位为保障自身生产经营活动的顺利进行，可以对劳动者违反企业劳动规章制度的行为进行制裁。

（　　）

30. 集体合同是指工会与用人单位或团体根据法律法规、规章的规定，就劳动报酬、工作时间、休息休假、劳动安全卫生等事项，通过集体协商签订的书面协议。

（　　）

31. 集体协商又称集体谈判，是用人单位工会或者职工代表与相应的用人单位代表为签订集体合同进行商谈的行为。

（　　）

32. 集体协商的首席代表可以由非本单位人员代理。

（　　）

33. 集体合同当事人双方的义务具有不对等性。

（　　）

34. 职工一方的协商代表由本单位工会选派，未建立工会的，需先成立工会。

（　　）

35. 劳动合同法第三十五条规定：职工个人与企业订立的劳动合同中劳动条件和劳动报酬等标准不得高于集体合同的规定。

（　　）

36. 集体合同是要式合同，是指合同必须按照双方约定的形式、内容和程序签订。

（　　）

37. 集体合同效力一般等同于劳动合同效力。

（　　）

38. 集体合同的主件是专项集体合同，是就劳动关系的某一特定方面的事项签订的专项协议。

（　　）

39. 签订集体合同过程中，劳动关系双方法律地位平等是集体合同订立的合法性原则。

（　　）

40. 用人单位因被兼并、解散、破产等原因，致使集体合同或专业集体合同无法履行的，经双方协商一致可以变更或解除集体合同。

（　　）

41. 2012 年 12 月中共中央纪委等六部门共同颁布《企业民主管理规定》，它是我国第一次以规章的形式全面规范以职工代表大会为基本形式的企业民主管理制度。

（　　）

42. 集体合同争议又称集体合同纠纷，是集体合同当事人因签订或履行集体合同而发生的争议。

（　　）

43. 协商是处理集体合同争议的必经程序。

（　　）

44. 当事人申请仲裁后，对仲裁不服的，可自收到仲裁裁决书之日起 10 日内向人民法院提起诉讼。

（　　）

45. 职工民主管理又称企业民主管理，指劳动者直接或间接参与管理所在企业内部事务，主要形式包括职工大会、职工代表大会或其他形式。

（　　）

46. 集体合同订立后，应当报送劳动行政部门，劳动行政部门自收到集体合同文本之日起 10 日内未提出异议的，集体合同即行生效。

（　　）

47. 工会的职责主要包括参与和协助。

（　　）

48. 组织参与和代表参与是职工民主管理的直接形式，岗位参与和个人参与是职工民主管理的间接形式。

（　　）

49. 目前我国的职工民主管理仅限于公有制企业。

（　　）

50. 职工代表大会依法行使的职权包括审议建议、审议通过、民主评议等。

（　　）

51. 职工代表大会制度是我国国有企业实行企业民主的最基本形式。

（　　）

52. 工会各级组织按照民主集中制原则建立。

（　　）

53. 工会成员不足 25 人的，不可以单独建立基层工会委员会，而需由几个单位联合组建基层工会委员会。

（　　）

54. 工会是职工自愿结合的工人阶级的群众组织，其基本职责是维护职工合法权益。

（　　）

55. 工会是依法建立的社会组织，国家保护其合法权益，任何组织和个人不得随意撤销、合并工会组织。

（　　）

56. 因履行集体合同发生争议，当事人协商不成的，可以向劳动行政部门申请仲裁。

（　　）

57. 企业民主管理具有两层含义：一是劳动者扮演管理者与决策者的角色参与企业的决策及管理，二是通过民主管理获得自身权益的保障。

（　　）

58. 当基层工会所在的企业关闭、合并或者破产及其他形式的企业终止，以及所在的机关、事业单位被撤销时，基层工会组织可以撤销。

（　　）

59. 工会经费的来源主要是工会会员缴纳的会费。

（　　）

60. 对于跨地区、跨行业的大型集团企业，中高层管理人员在职工代表中的占比不超过20%。

（　　）

二、单项选择题（下列每题的选项中，只有1个是正确的）

1. 从狭义上讲，（　　）就是企业与员工的沟通管理。

A. 劳动关系管理

B. 员工纪律管理

C. 员工关系管理

D. 员工情绪管理

2. （　　　）是员工关系管理的主要载体，体现一种文本形态。

A. 员工手册

B. 规章制度

C. 劳动合同

D. 集体合同

3. 员工上岗和离职面谈，人事手续办理，员工申诉和人事纠纷等相关劳动争议处理，属于员工关系管理的（　　　）。

A. 劳动关系管理

B. 员工纪律管理

C. 员工人际关系管理

D. 员工绩效管理

4. 员工手册涵盖了多个方面的内容，主要是企业各方面的（　　　）。

A. 管理制度

B. 民主管理制度

C. 安全卫生制度

D. 劳动规章制度

5. 劳动规章制度是（　　　）在劳动过程中的行为规则。

A. 劳动部门与劳动者

B. 职工与用人单位

C. 工会与劳动者

D. 劳动部门与用人单位

6. 企业制定劳动规章制度的权利由（　　　）授予。

A. 劳动部门

B. 董事会

C. 工会

D. 国家法律法规依法

7. （　　　）不是劳动规章制度的特点。

A. 法定授予性

B. 准立法性

C. 特定性

D. 契约性

8. 劳动规章制度的内容一般包括劳动条件、劳动纪律与（　　　）三大类。

A. 人事程序管理规定

B. 劳动报酬

C. 劳动安全

D. 劳动环境

9. 劳动规章制度不得违反劳动合同和（　　　）的约定。

A. 企业管理制度

B. 集体合同

C. 员工手册

D. 民主管理制度

10. （　　　）是劳动者与用人单位就劳动权利和义务达成的协议，如不违反法律法规，一经订立就具有法律约束力。

A. 劳动规章制度

B. 劳动纪律

C. 劳动合同

D. 集体合同

11. 劳动纪律是用人单位依法制定的、（　　　）在劳动过程中必须遵守的行为规则。

A. 用人单位

B. 全体职工

C. 职工与用人单位

D. 劳动部门与劳动者

12. （ ） 企业内部劳动规章制度，对职工不具有约束力。

A. 报送审查或备案的

B. 职工参与制定的

C. 未经公示的

D. 对员工有过培训并有书面记录的

13. （ ） 不是制定劳动纪律的原则。

A. 合法原则

B. 权责平等原则

C. 全面系统原则

D. 公平平等原则

14. 某企业规定，员工见到上级不主动打招呼的，可处以警告直至扣奖金的处罚。这明显违反了（ ） 原则。

A. 合法性

B. 合理性

C. 全面系统性

D. 公平公正性

15. 集体协商双方代表人数应当对等，每方至少（ ） 人，并确定一名首席代表。

A. 2

B. 3

C. 4

D. 5

16. 组织员工满意度调查，预防及处理员工消极怠工，解决员工关心的问题，属于员工关系管理的（　　）。

A. 员工情绪管理

B. 员工纪律管理

C. 员工人际关系管理

D. 员工绩效管理

17. （　　）是集体合同区别于一般民事、经济合同的一个重要特征。

A. 集体合同当事人双方的义务具有不对等性

B. 集体合同是要式合同

C. 集体合同当事人是特定的团体

D. 集体合同是集体性质的劳动协议

18. 集体合同或专项集体合同期限一般为（　　）。

A. 1 年

B. 2 年

C. 1~3 年

D. 1~5 年

19. 集体合同或专项集体合同签订或变更后应当自双方首席代表签字之日（　　），由用人单位一方将文本一式三份报送劳动保障行政部门审查。

A. 1 周内

B. 10 日内

C. 2 周内

D. 1 个月内

20. （　　）是企业依法制定的，企业员工在劳动过程中必须遵守的行为准则。

A. 劳动合同

B. 劳动纪律

C. 劳动时间

D. 劳动规范

21.（　　）不适合作为规章制度的公示方法。

A. 将劳动规章制度作为劳动合同的组成部分

B. 将企业劳动规章制度向每位入职员工发放

C. 以电子邮件和书面公告方式向全体员工公示

D. 由部门经理向员工进行传达

22. 劳动法规定：职工个人与企业订立的劳动合同中，（　　）等标准不得低于集体合同的规定。

A. 劳动条件和劳动报酬

B. 劳动条件和劳动时间

C. 劳动报酬和劳动时间

D. 劳动时间和劳动环境

23. 集体协商双方首席代表可以书面委托本单位以外的专业人员作为本方协商代表，委托人数不得超过本方代表的（　　）。

A. 1/2

B. 1/3

C. 1/4

D. 1/5

24. 劳动合同的签约双方主体是（　　）。

A. 劳动行政部门和劳动者

B. 工会和劳动者

C. 用人单位和劳动者

D. 用人单位和劳动行政部门

25. 仲裁委员会自收到集体合同申诉书之日起（　　　）内做出受理或不受理决定。

　　A. 3 日

　　B. 10 日

　　C. 15 日

　　D. 30 日

26. 在解除劳动合同时，只有当（　　　）发生时，企业可以不支付经济补偿金。

　　A. 经劳动合同当事人协商一致，由企业解除劳动合同

　　B. 非因企业过错由劳动者主动提出解除劳动合同

　　C. 劳动者经培训或者调整工作岗位仍不能胜任工作而解除劳动合同

　　D. 劳动者患病，医疗期满后不能从事原工作也不能从事企业另行安排的新工作而解除劳动合同

27. 集体合同草案或专项集体合同草案应提交职工代表大会或全体职工讨论，应当有（　　　）以上职工代表或职工出席。

　　A. 1/2

　　B. 1/3

　　C. 2/3

　　D. 1/4

28. 集体合同或专项集体合同期满前（　　　）内，任何一方均可向对方提出重新签订或续订要求。

　　A. 2 个月

　　B. 3 个月

C. 6 个月

D. 1 个月

29. 特别仲裁庭一般由（　　）组成。

A. 2 个以上单数仲裁员

B. 3 个以上单数仲裁员

C. 2 个以上双数仲裁员

D. 3 个以上双数仲裁员

30. 当事人申请仲裁后，对仲裁不服的，可自收到仲裁裁决书之日起（　　）内向人民法院提起诉讼。

A. 3 日

B. 7 日

C. 15 日

D. 30 日

31. 劳动行政部门对集体合同或专项集体合同有异议的，应当自收到文本之日起（　　）将"审查意见书"送达双方协商代表。

A. 7 日内

B. 15 日内

C. 20 日内

D. 30 日内

32. 如果劳动规章制度与劳动合同冲突或不一致，除非（　　）认可，否则无效。

A. 劳动者

B. 工会

C. 人力资源部门

D. 职工代表大会

33. 集体协商是用人单位工会或主管代表与相应的用人单位代表为签订（   ）进行商谈的行为。

A. 集体合同

B. 劳动合同

C. 经济合同

D. 民事合同

34. （   ）不得由非本单位人员代理。

A. 集体协商的首席代表

B. 用人单位协商代表

C. 职工协商代表

D. 工会主席

35. 签订集体合同必须兼顾双方的合法权益，这也是（   ）的要求。

A. 系统原则

B. 公平原则

C. 合法原则

D. 计划原则

36. 劳动行政部门自收到集体合同文本之日起（   ）日内未提出异议的，集体合同或专项集体合同即行生效。

A. 3

B. 10

C. 15

D. 30

37. （   ）我国第一次以规章的形式全面规范以职工代表大会为基本形式的企业民主管理制度。

A. 2010 年

B. 2011 年

C. 2012 年

D. 2013 年

38. 用人单位需要职工代表大会审议建议的事项为（　　）。

A. 集体合同草案

B. 群体性劳动纠纷进行集体协商

C. 薪酬制度

D. 劳动用工管理制度

39. 用人单位需要职工代表大会审议通过的事项为（　　）。

A. 企业财务预决算

B. 集体合同草案

C. 企业重组改制方案

D. 工会与企业就职工工资调整进行集体协商

40. （　　）是民主管理制度的直接形式。

A. 组织参与和代表参与

B. 岗位参与和个人参与

C. 组织参与和岗位参与

D. 个人参与和代表参与

41. （　　）是企业内部组织机构的重要组成部分。

A. 工会

B. 职工民主管理制度

C. 劳动规章制度

D. 职工代表大会制度

42. 集体合同的签约双方主体可以是（　　）。

A. 劳动行政部门和劳动者

B. 工会和劳动者

C. 工会与用人单位

D. 用人单位和劳动行政部门

43. 企业、事业、机关建立基层工会委员会的条件是工会会员（　　　）以上。

A. 20 人

B. 25 人

C. 30 人

D. 35 人

44. 劳动合同中不得约定试用期的情形是（　　　）。

A. 劳动合同期限不满三个月

B. 无固定期限劳动合同

C. 一年以上劳动合同

D. 三年以上劳动合同

45. （　　　）是指在签约集体合同过程中，劳动关系双方法律地位平等。

A. 双赢性

B. 自愿性

C. 契约性

D. 合作性

46. （　　　）是处理集体合同争议的必经程序。

A. 协商

B. 仲裁

C. 诉讼

D. 判决

47. （　　　）是工会的基本职责。

A. 工会的参与职能

B. 工会的协助职能

C. 协商劳动关系

D. 代表和维护职工权益

48. 工会经费的来源之一是建立工会组织的企业、事业单位、机关按每月全部职工工资总额的（　　　）向工会拨缴的经费。

A. 2%

B. 3%

C. 4%

D. 5%

49. 新建工程的职业安全卫生设施必须与主体工程（　　　）、同时施工、同时投入生产和使用。

A. 同时设计

B. 同时审查

C. 同时验收

D. 同时登记

50. 基层工会组织可以撤销，撤销时应当报告（　　　）。

A. 董事会

B. 劳动行政管理部门

C. 上一级工会

D. 职工代表大会

51. 集体合同签订或变更后，应自双方首席代表签字之日起（　　　）内，由用人单位一方将文本一式（　　　）报送劳动行政部门审查。

A. 3 日；1 份

B. 7 日；2 份

C. 10 日；3 份

D. 15 日；3 份

52. （　　）不属于可以撤销基层工会组织的情况。

A. 所在的企业关闭、合并

B. 所在企业破产

C. 所在的机关、事业单位被撤销

D. 工会成员下降到法定数量以下

53. （　　）不是工会的建议权所涉及的范畴。

A. 企业单方面解除职工劳动合同时

B. 涉及劳动安全卫生权利

C. 停工怠工事件

D. 涉及员工奖惩处罚

54. 对生效的集体合同要报（　　）备案。

A. 上级工会部门

B. 劳动行政部门

C. 劳动争议仲裁委员会

D. 人民法院

55. 集体协商时，职工一方的协商代表，由（　　）选派。

A. 上级工会部门

B. 劳动行政部门

C. 本单位行政部门

D. 本单位工会

56.《中华人民共和国劳动法》和《中华人民共和国劳动合同法》就集体合同的可备条款做出了不完全列举规定，2004 年修订的《集体合同规定》明确规定的为（　　）项内容。

A. 5

B. 10

C. 15

D. 20

57. 我国现行有效法律规范对惩戒处分依据的法规是《中华人民共和国劳动法》和（   ）。

A. 劳动者过错导致用人单位单方解除劳动合同的规定

B. 劳动手册

C. 中华人民共和国劳动合同法

D. 关于用人单位规章制度的规定

58. 现行职工民主管理的形式主要有组织参与、代表参与、（   ）和个人参与。

A. 集体参与

B. 部门参与

C. 高层参与

D. 工会参与

59. 企业单方面解除职工劳动合同时，应当事先将理由通知（   ）。

A. 职工代表大会

B. 工会

C. 劳动者

D. 职工所在部门

三、多项选择题（下列每题的选项中，至少有 2 个是正确的）

1. 员工关系管理有利于（   ）。

A. 协调和改善企业内部人际关系

B. 树立员工的团体价值

C. 增强企业对员工的凝聚力

D. 激励员工的工作积极性

2. 企业劳动规章制度的特征主要表现在（   ）。

A. 特定性

B. 立法性

C. 契约性

D. 法定授予性

3. 企业有效的劳动规章制度所应该具备的要件是（   ）。

A. 企业劳动规章制度的法律效力不能溯及以往

B. 必须是由用人单位依法制定

C. 必须公示明确告知劳动者规章的内容

D. 劳动规章制度不得违反劳动合同和集体合同的约定

4. （   ）的劳动规章制度在劳动争议处理中可发挥举证作用。

A. 用人单位单方制定

B. 必须是由用人单位依法制定

C. 必须公示并明确告知劳动者

D. 职工参与制定

5. 劳动纪律制定原则（   ）。

A. 合法原则

B. 全面履行原则

C. 全面系统原则

D. 公平平等原则

6. 从管理职责来看，员工关系管理主要有（   ）等内容。

A. 劳动关系管理

B. 员工纪律管理

C. 员工人际关系管理

D. 员工绩效管理

7. 员工手册编写的原则包括（　　）等。

A. 企业文化

B. 组织结构

C. 人事制度

D. 行为规范

8. 集体合同与劳动合同的区别（　　）。

A. 签订合同的主体不同

B. 订立合同的目的不同

C. 两者的效力不同

D. 合同内容不同

9. 集体合同除具备一般合同的共同特征外，还具有（　　）等特征。

A. 集体合同是集体性质的劳动协议

B. 集体合同的当事人双方的义务具有对等性

C. 集体合同是要式合同

D. 集体合同的效力高于劳动合同

10. 集体合同是工会与用人单位就（　　）等事项签订的书面协议。

A. 劳动报酬

B. 工作时间

C. 福利津贴

D. 职位升迁

11. 订立集体合同应该遵循的原则包括（　　）。

A. 合法性

B. 自愿性

C. 权利义务对等性

D. 双赢性

E. 和谐性

12. 员工手册的基本内容包括企业概况（　　　）。

A. 企业文化

B. 组织结构

C. 人事制度

D. 行为规范

13. 集体协商的技巧包括（　　　）。

A. 做好谈判准备工作

B. 制定谈判策略，建立信任关系

C. 语言的运用

D. 增强耐心与自信

14. （　　　）是职工民主管理的形式。

A. 组织参与

B. 岗位参与

C. 代表参与

D. 集体参与

E. 个人参与

15. （　　　）是工会的职责。

A. 参与职能

B. 审查监督

C. 审议建议

D. 协助职能

16. 工会有权对职业安全卫生设施的"三同时"即（   ）进行监督。

A. 同时设计

B. 同时施工

C. 同时审查

D. 同时投产使用

17. （   ）并存，共同执行着协调劳动关系的职能。

A. 劳动规章制度

B. 职工民主管理制度

C. 劳动合同制度

D. 集体合同制度

E. 劳动争议处理制度

18. 劳动者过错导致用人单位单方解除劳动合同的情形（   ）。

A. 严重违反用人单位的规章制度的

B. 劳动者不能胜任工作，经培训或者调整工作岗位仍不能胜任工作的

C. 劳动者严重失职，给用人单位造成重大损失的

D. 劳动者患病，在规定的医疗期的

E. 劳动者同时与其他用人单位建立劳动关系，对完成本单位的工作任务造成严重影响，或者经用人单位提出，拒不改正的

19. 企业职工一方与用人单位通过平等协商，可以就（   ）事项订立集体合同。

A. 劳动报酬

B. 工作时间

C. 休息休假

D. 劳动安全卫生

E. 保险福利

20. 集体协商代表的（　　　）是协商成功的关键因素之一。

A. 职位

B. 知识

C. 经验

D. 能力

E. 年龄

21. 职工代表大会具有（　　　）特点。

A. 是企业重要的管理机构

B. 广泛的代表性和充分的民主性

C. 是企业内部组织机构的重要组成部分

D. 是企业实行民主管理的基本形式

实务技能单元测试题

第一篇 人力资源规划

一、项目策划（1~2题，每题30分，共60分）

1. 背景资料

某公司成立于 2012 年，由于经营有术，公司迅猛发展的同时，也暴露了很多问题，如人员紧张，部门职责不清等。人力资源部经理把王亮叫到办公室："你是我们部门唯一学管理的研究生，我决定由你来系统地做一下工作分析，以明确每个岗位的工作职责。"

王亮先是查看了公司现有的工作说明书，发现存在这样几个问题：格式过于简单、内容不完整、描述不准确，有些内容过时等。于是，王亮不再依赖原有文件，开始竭尽所能地收集有关资料，向人力资源部经理请教，弄清新的组织架构，然后利用网络查询与每个职位有关的信息，并依据自己的理解进行信息的取舍。最后完成了工作分析，并形成了各职位的工作说明书。

尽管王亮花了大量的时间和精力进行工作分析，但公司各岗位职责不清的现象仍未得到很好的改善。

问题：

1. 该公司在进行工作分析中存在什么问题？（15 分）

2. 如果你是王亮，你将如何进行工作分析？（15 分）

2. 背景资料

某绿色化工公司为了进一步发展，制定了五年战略发展增长目标，规划在新的业务领域开发出几种有吸引力的新产品，期望公司销售额五年内翻一番。为了适应公司整体发展战略的要求，人力资源部开始着手准备公司未来五年的人力资源规划。

公司目前共有生产与维修工人825人，行政和文秘143人，中层管理人员79人，设计和产品研发人员38人，销售人员23人。近五年来员工的离职率为14％，不同类别的员工的离职率不一样，其中设计与研发人员流失率较高，达20％以上。

在进行人力资源需求分析时，人力资源部听取了现在各部门负责人的想法。各部门负责人为使自己部门将来的人手能够充足，纷纷强调自己部门的重要性，提出了很多要求，包括人数和人员层次等方面。人力资源部基于这些数据汇编成了公司未来的人力资源需求表，却发现庞大的人员需求量是公司难以承受的，也无法确定如何才能落实未来的人才落地措施。

问题：

1. 你认为该公司人力资源需求预测中存在什么问题？（14 分）

2. 如何进行公司人力资源需求预测，具体内容有哪些？（16 分）

二、案例分析题（3～4题，每题20分，共40分）

3. 背景资料

怡丽服装公司是一家集研发设计、生产和销售为一体的服装制品公司，成立于2008年，经过几年的努力，公司获得了快速发展。

从2012年开始，公司业务逐步繁忙起来，经常出现人手不够的情况，特别是管理人才严重不足。时常新的项目来了，才开始招聘人员，企业招聘也没有规范的流程，拿到碗里就是菜。员工录取后，马上到生产一线开始工作。在试用期，员工的离职率特别高，近几年这种局面和现状一直没有改变，对公司的业务发展造成了一定的不利影响。

问题：

1. 该公司在人力资源管理方面存在什么问题？（8分）

2. 如果出现供小于求，你建议该公司采取哪些措施恢复平衡？（12分）

4. 背景资料

李涛是新上任的行政人事经理，财务部王经理和他说要招聘一名会计。李涛爽快地说：王经理，您写个招聘申请表把要求列出来，我马上安排人手给您物色人选。王经理诧异地说：招聘申请表是什么啊，没有见过啊！李涛马上猜想到了，估计公司没有这方面的人力资源表单。

小张生孩子了，工会主席来问李涛，说该出多少礼金为好？李涛很郁闷地问道："公司没有这方面的规章制度吗"。工会主席摇摇头：没有啊，以往都是我与人事经理商量好了，报给总经理审批。

月底，李涛在审核薪酬主管王晓玲制作的考勤表时问道：公司加班有申请手续吗？王晓玲说："以往都是部门经理自己记录本部门的加班情况，月底再汇总给我"。

李涛通过这一系列事件发现公司的人力资源管理制度非常薄弱，有些还是公司成立之初建立的，也有一些制度如绩效管理、培训等居然还在使用其他公司的，随着公司的快速发展，在员工管理中一旦出现问题，根本找不到相应的政策处理……于是，李涛决定重新编制公司的人力资源管理制度。

问题：

1. 该公司人力资源管理制度建设违背了哪些原则？（8分）

2. 如果要编制人力资源管理制度，李涛该如何操作？（12分）

第二篇　招聘与配置

一、项目策划（1~2题，每题30分，共60分）

1. 背景资料

　　小李是一位优秀的物流管理人才，有着多家大型快消品企业的物流管理经验。而且业绩突出，在业内享有盛名。

　　A公司是一家2003年10月注册成立的快速消费品生产和销售企业。由于产品独特，一投入市场，便有大批订单蜂拥而至。2004年入夏以来，随着业务量的激增，物流运转不够顺畅，物流成本不断增加，效率大打折扣，一些经销商的不满情绪渐增。在这种情况下，公司迫切需要一位优秀的物流管理人才。

　　此时，恰逢想换工作环境和希望接受挑战的小李前来应聘，人力资源部经理久闻小李大名，见机会难得，直接上报总裁。总裁求贤若渴，亲自上阵面试，经过交谈发现小李确实是自己梦寐以求的物流管理人才，于是当场拍板，让小李次日上班，担任物流部经理。

人力资源部经理和总裁如释重负。但是，3 个星期以后，两人却意外地收到了小李的辞呈。

经过多方了解，人力资源部经理弄清了小李离职的原因：①思想活跃、喜欢创新和挑战的小李与保守稳重的直接上级——生产副总多次因意见不统一而发生冲突；②小李在 A 公司物流部面对一群"素质不高"的同事，经常产生一种"曲高和寡"的孤独感；③小李无法适应一个各项制度不健全、管理流程混乱的企业，认为在这样的企业，自己的能力无从施展。

问题：

1. 小李的闪电离职令人深思，请分析 A 公司在招聘中存在什么问题？（12 分）

2. 如果你是人力资源主管，如何改进本职位的招聘？（18 分）

2. 背景资料

翔云公司是一家中型国有企业，是化学高分子材料制造行业的领头羊。近 5 年来，公司产品销售收入以 20% 的速度递增。然而，2016 年以来公司的产品销售收入却并不乐观，直至 6 月仅完成计划销售收入的 35%。公司对产品进行的市场调研显示，老产品所占据的市场份额已经到了顶峰，某些产品销售量甚至开始下滑；面临行业产品的快速更新换代，公司产品品种单一，新产品的研制和上市速度过慢。同时，大部分代理商也反映公司产品推新不够及时，老产品缺少市场前景。

与此同时，人力资源部接到了很多员工的辞职申请，主要是研发和销售人员，已经开始影响公司的业务了。为此，人力资源部决定进行离职面谈，并由人力资源部经理、薪酬主管和部门经理组成面谈小组，在公司会议室与近期要求离职的 15 名员工开展了每人 20 分钟的谈话，问了一些准备好的常规问题，主要听取大家离职的原因，但因为时间关系也未进行深入追问，更没有明确表示挽留。15 名员工几乎都讲是自己个人原因要求离职，本人对公司还是十分有感情的。

问题：

1. 翔云公司的离职面谈存在什么问题？（12 分）

2. 你认为该如何有效组织离职面谈？（18 分）

二、案例分析题（3～4 题，每题 20 分，共 40 分）

3. 背景资料

申宏计算机技术有限公司是一家专门从事软件开发、系统集成、计算机产品销售的企业。拥有 200 多名职工，企业年营业额达 10 亿元。最近公司准备招聘市场经理，主要从事网络产品的推广，工作中既需要与客户进行沟通，同时又要有相关的专业技术背景。公司借助广告媒介，发布了招聘信息，并收到了上百份简历，通过简历筛选后确定了 6 位候选人进入面试程序。采用面试方法对应聘者进行甄选。

通常这类面试都是由部门经理参与的，这两天部门经理出差，人力资源部觉得在技术方面张力还是不错的，于是临时邀请张力顶替参与本次招聘面试。

张力是 3 年前通过校园招聘进入公司的技术员，对于招聘面试毫无准备，也从没有担任过面试考官。来到面试现场后，张力紧张地翻阅着手中的面试打分表和候选人的自荐资料，做了一些面试前期准备，但面试打分表只有简单的指标名称，并没有具体的打分标准，对于如何打分，心里完全没底。在人力资源部的提醒和催促下，张力只能凭感觉对应聘者过去的技术经历作了一些提问与记录。很快，6名应聘者的面试结束了，张力也凭着自己的理解完成了打分。

问题：

1. 请分析该公司在招聘面试中存在哪些问题？（8分）

2. 你认为招聘面试准备阶段应有哪些工作？（12分）

4. 背景资料

胜华公司人力资源部招聘一名培训助理，培训主管从应聘资料中挑选了一位较为符合要求的应聘者进行了面试。下面是培训主管和这位应聘者进行面谈的摘录：

培训主管：请你介绍一下你之前做过哪些工作？

应聘者：我大学毕业后在一家公司做过两年培训助理，做的具体工作与你们在招聘启事上写得差不多。现在公司要搬迁到郊区，因为家里老小都要照顾，所以我想另外找一份合适的工作。

培训主管：虽然工作内容差不太多，都是做培训助理，但请你举一个实际做过的例子，让我能了解一下你的工作内容和范围。

应聘者：去年我们公司为了提高中层干部的管理理念和技能，组织了一次中层干部的管理培训，专门请某培训咨询公司进行设计与实施。我一直参与这个项目，直至培训项目最终结束。大家对这次培训的评价都非常好，总经理也很满意，我也从中学到了很多东西，尤其是在与培训公司交往和联系方面获得了不少经验，相信这些经验一定能在新的公司中发挥作用。

培训主管：某培训公司也为我们服务过，他们确实非常专业，相信你一定学到了很多东西。那我们再问问其他问题吧……

问题：

1. 培训主管运用的 STAR 原则具体包括哪些内容？（8 分）

2. 根据 STAR 原则，培训主管还可以对应聘者做哪些追问？（12 分）

第三篇　培训与开发

一、项目策划（1~2题，每题30分，共60分）

1. 背景资料

杉达公司是一家由国企改制为民营的制药企业，现有员工800人。为了能在激烈的竞争中站稳脚跟，公司总经理认识到培训的重要性，提取销售收入的3%用于员工的技能培训。虽然培训投入加大了，但总经理还是觉得公司绩效没怎么提高。

在新任人力资源经理的安排下，人力资源部对目前公司内部人员结构和过去的培训情况进行了初步分析，发现公司培训只有一些过程的时间安排表，以往的培训内容都是由人力资源部借鉴培训公司提供的培训课程确定的，培训经费主要运用在外部培训上，同时培训时间安排比较混乱，常常迁就培训师，导致有些培训课程时间安排不合理。在实施培训过程中，各部门经理根据工作忙闲程度选派工作量较少的人员参加培训，员工也普遍感觉培训对自己的工作能力提升不大，而有些重要的技能没有进行培训。为此，人力资源经理要求培训主管拿出改善方案，以提高培训的效果。

问题：

1. 杉达公司培训管理中存在哪些问题？（12 分）

2. 如果你是该公司的培训主管，你将如何进行培训需求调查。（18 分）

2. 背景资料

李墨妍是人力资源专业的研究生，毕业后，在朋友的介绍下进入中华家用电器制造公司，在人力资源部担任培训师。中华家用电器公司是一家大型家用电器生产企业，下辖 7 个分厂，分别从事各种零件的制造和生产装配业务。一年后，李墨妍被总公司调到公司最大的零件制造 5 厂担任人力资源部经理助理，专门负责员工培训和开发工作。两年后被提升为 5 厂人力资源部经理，目前他在这一职位上工作了将近 4 年。由于总公司人事调整，这个任期结束，李墨妍将被调到公司总部，担任总公司员工培训与开发经理助理。

中华家用电器公司计划 12 个月内在苏州开设一家新的分厂，新厂计划用 3 年时间雇佣 1200 名员工。在新分厂开业的时候，大约只能雇佣到 1/3 的员工，剩下的员工只能在开业后的 2 年内招募到位。由于这个分厂的规模与李墨妍目前所在的分厂不相上下，只是生产工艺和设备比较先进。因此，总公司要求他提供一份新工厂员工培训方案。

根据总公司的决策，新工厂的所有中高层管理人员，将从其他 7 个分厂的员工中选拔，对这些人来说将是一次提升。而所有这些被选拔出来的管理人员都要由总公司进行培训，由李墨妍负责。在新厂开业的时候，这些管理人员都必须到位。

问题：

1. 根据公司规定，此次新员工培训时间为 1 个月，包括 1 周军训和相关

179

课程培训（课程培训的讲师部分外请，场地为公司培训中心），费用约为12万元。培训活动在开展之前人力资源部要向上级编报培训预算方案，根据提供的材料，请为李墨妍编制一个培训费用预算申报表并做相应说明，包括费用类型和所占比例等。（12分）

2. 如果你是人力资源主管，如何有效地进行培训组织的实施？（18分）

二、案例分析题（3~4题，每题20分，共40分）

3. 背景资料

腾云公司是从事日用品销售的企业，多年来在行业内享有很高的信誉。公司管理者关于培训工作持有这样一些观点；培训旨在提高公司核心竞争力，是企业的战略，既然企业花了大钱，员工就必须无条件接受；岗位工作很重要，培训不应影响日常工作，但凡培训应该安排在下班时间或双休日时间；公司会周期性安排外聘专家进行理论强化，同时为了培养复合人才，主张跨专业培训学习；强调新员工和老员工应一视同仁，统一参加培训课程；公司要求所有员工线上学习，显示公司现代化管理的水平。公司要求一线销售员工、职能管理部门员工、中层管理者必须通过公司全年全员培训课程。

按照这样的思路实施培训管理，员工普遍反映，由于培训课程过多，信息量过大，员工反而对于公司未来产品的定位、企业发展方向和自己职业生涯产生了困惑。

问题：

1. 腾云公司员工培训中主要存在哪些问题？（8分）

2. 如果你是人力资源主管在制订培训计划时应明确哪些内容？（12分）

4. 背景资料

理想公司的培训主管小杨在看到国外许多 e‐Learning 的成功案例后，决定替公司导入 e‐Learning，开始在线培训。小杨在询问了公司的信息部门后，开始采购线上教学平台，用以处理线上课程开课时的相关事宜。小杨委托软件咨询公司对各类 e‐Learning 教学平台进行了功能的评估，并最终结合评估报告完成了教学平台的采购。3 个月后，教学平台顺利建立起来了，小杨高兴地向总经理汇报：我们企业已有 e‐Learning 了。

于是小杨开始将内部的文件与教材规划上线，但他发现，原来线上课程的设计制作不是那么简单的！尽管已经把文件和档案放在了平台上，但学员的浏览和学习意愿却始终不高。学员希望课程必须符合有趣、互动、多媒体等特性。要自己制作设计课程，没那么多时间；若找厂商制作，花费大笔财力不说，课程的设计又无法兼顾学习重点。半年之后，小杨发现e‐Learning 不但未能替企业省钱，反而花了更多的人力与预算去推动，于是只能禀告总经理将 e‐Learning 计划暂时搁置。

问题：

1. 理想公司 e‐Learning 失败的原因是什么？（8 分）

2. 选择科学的培训方法应注意哪些环节？（12 分）

第四篇　绩效管理

一、项目策划（1~2题，每题30分，共60分）

1. 背景资料

某地产公司专注于开发及经营高质量、大规模、多业态的综合性商业地产项目，公司现有50个物业项目，其中26个项目是城市综合体。

为了进一步增强公司的竞争力，公司开始重视人力资源管理，并决定从年底开始实施绩效评估，因为年底的绩效评估与奖金挂钩，大家都非常重视。人力资源部将一些考评表发到各部门经理的手中，要求部门经理在规定的时间内填写完表格，再交回人力资源部。人力资源部以此作为最终的评价结果，并作为发奖金的依据。李良是销售部经理，拿到人力资源部送来的考评表格，却不知怎么办。表格主要包括了对员工工作业绩和工作态度的评价。工作业绩那栏分为五个档，每档只有简短的评语。年初由于种种原因，李经理没有将员工的业绩指标清楚地确定下来。因此对业绩考评时，无法判断谁超额完成任务，谁没有完成任务。工作态度就更难填写了，由于平时没有收集和记录员工的工作表现，到了年底，只对近一两个月的事情有点记忆。

问题：

1. 该公司在绩效评估中存在哪些问题？（10分）

2. 请为该公司策划销售岗位的绩效指标设计流程。（20分）

2. 背景资料

海申公司是由海外留学归来的3位同学创立的电脑配件制造企业。自2005年建厂以来经济效益一直很好，每年的利润以两位数递增。近期，由于市场竞争激烈，国内同类企业数量的不断增加，经济效益、利润滑坡严重，员工的收入也受到影响，队伍不稳定，流失率高达25%以上。2016年春节后，公司高层参观学习了同行业3个标杆企业。回公司以后，大家都对标杆企业的绩效管理留下了深刻印象，认为应该学习。

公司高层决定，绩效管理由人力资源部全面负责，要求在2周内拿出绩效计划，1个月内公司全面推广。为此，人力资源部召开了部门经理会议，希望确定公司的绩效计划。但在开会当天，已经过了开会时间，部门经理们才姗姗到来。在会上，人力资源经理仔细讲解了绩效计划的要求，希望各部门一起参与，但大家似听非听、似懂非懂，私下里窃窃私语，觉得这个绩效计划应该是人力资源部的事情。最后，在问大家有没有意见时，经理们都认为现在业务很忙，没有时间讨论研究，不如人力资源部直接做一个绩效计划，大家按照执行就行了。会后，人力资源部要求陆丽负责绩效计划的编制。为了抢时间，陆丽参照了标杆企业的绩效计划，根据总经理的要求，编制了绩效计划和实施方案，提交给总经理审核确定，最终在两周内完成了绩效计划的编制，并作为本年度绩效管理的文件下发给各部门进行实施。

问题：

1. 该公司在绩效计划制订过程中违反了哪些原则？（15分）

2. 如果你是人力资源主管，将如何进行绩效计划的制订？（15分）

二、案例分析题（3～4题，每题20分，共40分）

3. 背景资料

刘明是某企业生产部门的主管，今天他终于费尽心思地完成了对下属人员的绩效考核，并准备把考核表交给人力资源部。绩效考核表格中表明了员工工作的数量和质量以及合作态度等情况，表中的每一个要素都分为五等：优秀、良好、一般、及格和不及格。所有的员工都完成了本职工作，除了 X 和 Y，大部分顺利完成了 Z 交给的额外工作。

考虑到 A 和 B 是新员工，他们两人的额外工作量又偏多，Z 给他们的工作都打了"优秀"。C 曾经对 Z 做出的一个决定表示过不同意见，在"合作态度"一栏，被记为"一般"，因为意见分歧只是工作方式方面的问题，所以 Z 没有在表格的评价栏上做记录。另外，D 家庭比较困难，Z 就有意识地提高了对他的评价，他想通过这种方式让 D 多拿绩效工资，把帮助落到实处。此外，E 的工作质量不好，也就是及格，但为避免难堪，Z 把他的评价提到"一般"。这样，员工的评价分布于"优秀"、"良好"、"一般"，就没有"及格"和"不及格"了。Z 觉得这样做，可以使员工不至于因发现绩效考核低而不满；同时，上级考评时，自己的下级工作做得好，对自己的绩效考核，成绩也差不了。

问题:

1. 请从过程组织的角度分析本次绩效评估存在哪些问题?(8 分)

2. 你认为该公司应如何改进绩效评估过程组织?(12 分)

4. 背景资料

王峰在一家民营公司做基层主管已经有 3 年了。去年公司开始进行绩效管理,员工们也开始知道了一些有关绩效考核的具体要求。

今年春节前,王峰的上司刘经理同他进行了绩效考核的谈话,王峰很是不安。虽然他对过去一年的工作比较满意,但日常工作中与刘经理的沟通不多。在绩效反馈的谈话中,刘经理对王峰的表现总体是肯定的,指出了他性格上的一些问题,如比较内向,与领导沟通不够主动,做事效率不是很高等。王峰也同意那些看法。由于刘经理有事,整个谈话只进行了 10 分钟左右,王峰也没有机会表达自己的想法,对工作中曾产生的一些误会没来得及反馈,对一些工作中的困惑和改进的方法也未交流。但离开刘经理办公室时,感觉整个谈话过程是令人愉快的,觉得自己今年的绩效成绩应该不错。

但当王峰拿到上司给他的年终考评书面报告时,王峰感到震惊,书面报告写了他在工作中的不少问题,而他的成绩和优点只稍微描述了几句。书面报告所描述的具体问题在绩效反馈沟通中根本没有提到,有些问题也和实际情况存在出入,王峰觉得这样的结果好像有点“不可理喻”和无法接受,王峰很苦恼。

问题:

1. 你认为刘经理在本次绩效结果反馈时未能遵循哪些原则?(9 分)

2. 你建议刘经理该如何改进绩效结果反馈?(11 分)

第五篇　薪酬与福利管理

一、项目策划 (1~2题，每题30分，共60分)

1. 背景资料

盛业公司虽然是刚成立不满5年的民营企业，但由于管理有方，已成为国内生产规模最大、技术实力最强的电子产品公司。

公司成立之初，曾以完善的培训体系，富有竞争力的薪酬福利吸引了大批人才的加入，帮助企业迅速崛起。但近两年来，公司内部却出现了核心员工离职率大幅上升，同时也影响了在岗员工的情绪，公司产品研发和创新能力大为降低，连续两年基本上无新产品上市，今年初，公司市场份额已下滑到行业第三。

公司李总非常着急，找来人力资源部门商量对策。人力资源部门发现，员工的不满主要集中在薪酬问题上。研发部原来的经理离职后在新公司的薪酬差不多，员工也反映公司薪酬增幅太慢，销售部的人员也总是抱怨他们拼死拼活在推销产品，薪酬和那些坐在办公室里没事干的行政人员差不多。随即，李总指示人力资源部门进行薪酬体系的改革。

问题：

1. 该公司的薪酬体系存在什么问题？（12 分）

2. 基于本案例，你将如何进行该公司的薪酬调查？（18 分）

2. 背景资料

大地公司是一家营销型企业，营销人员是公司的主要员工，公司为他们专门设计了"底薪＋佣金制"的薪酬模式，从而降低了企业对营销人员薪酬支付风险。然而，公司的营销网络在很大程度与个人而不是与品牌相关联，这对企业来说存在着很大的用人隐患，一旦有关键员工离开，公司营销网络有可能遭受重大损失的风险。因此，大地公司通过几年的发展，在积累了一定的经济实力后，制定了高于市场薪酬标准的薪酬制度，招聘并组建了一支以博士和硕士为主体的研发团队，公司设想通过建设品牌营销来逐步替代个人魅力营销现状。

由于公司研发团队艰辛付出，取得了卓越成果，大地公司的品牌迅速在市场上打响，产品销售非常火爆，公司也逐步成长为集研发、生产和营销为一体的集团性企业。

然而，因大地公司营销团队实行的是"底薪＋佣金制"的薪酬模式，对大部分营销人员来说，由于研发团队研发出的产品好销，不用费太大的努力就可以取得较好的业绩，拿到高额佣金。而研发人员虽然是高薪酬，但绩效薪酬并不高，薪酬收入有时还不如营销人员。这引起了研发团队的强烈不满，甚至个别研发人员认为公司不重视智力成果，愤然辞职离去。

大地公司经营管理层清醒地意识到，有必要对公司的薪酬制度进行重新设计和调整。

问题：

1. 大地公司薪酬结构设计时违背了哪些原则？（12分）

2. 进行薪酬调整要开展哪些工作？（18分）

二、案例分析题（3～4题，每题20分，共40分）

3. 背景资料

建业公司是一家生产、研发电子控制系统的高科技企业，多年来和高校以及研究所合作，引入多个专利项目，然后再做二次开发。公司从2008年初10个人成立的小公司，快速成长为规模达400人的企业，创业之初的人员现在都是各部门的领导，公司已经度过了创业初期的不稳定阶段，正在向更好的轨道发展。

随着公司业务的不断发展，人员的需求进一步增加。但公司人力资源部反映，目前很难招聘到公司需要的技术人员。生产线的员工流动性目前也偏高，有时一个月的流失率就达20%。分析其原因，主要归结为公司的薪酬制度不具备竞争力。目前公司薪酬结构分为三块：基本薪酬、岗位津贴、绩效工资。按岗位技能（工作难易）设计并采用了岗位技能工资制。生产线员工的基本薪酬2000元/月，技术人员基本薪酬3200元/月。岗位津贴按工作环境和级别分为：一线员工200元/月、技术人员初级180元/月、技术人员中级250元/月、技术人员高级400元/月。奖金按基本薪酬的10%计提，主要按出勤率予以考核。据相关调查资料显示，公司的薪酬水平处于市场同行水平的35%。人力资源部经理建议改革公司的薪酬，适当提高公司薪酬水平，调整薪资结构，以适应市场的要求。公司领导采纳了该建议，要求人力资源部尽快拿出薪酬改革方案。

问题：

1. 建业公司原有薪酬结构在设计上存在的主要问题是什么？（10分）

2. 为了提升公司薪酬竞争力，你将如何开展岗位评价？（10分）

4. 背景资料

星宇公司是一个营销型企业，早期公司的营销网络在很大程度与个人而不是与品牌相关联，这对于企业来说存在着很大的用人隐患。为此，公司通过几年的发展在积累了一定的经济实力后，招聘并组建了一支以博士和硕士为主的研发团队，制定了高于市场薪酬标准的薪酬制度，薪酬结构是"基本工资＋效益工资"。效益工资在整个工资结构中占比很低，仅为10%，基本工资很高，在市场销售不确定的情况下，保障了研发人员的稳定性和安全感。由于公司研发团队艰辛付出，取得了卓越成果，星宇公司的品牌迅速在市场上打响，产品销售非常火爆。

但在近期，管理层发现研发人员的工作主动性有所不足，忠诚度有所下降，新产品研发的周期变长，研发人员陆续有人离职，还有不少人蠢蠢欲动。通过调查发现，研究人员认为，公司产品销售火爆，企业利润丰厚，但他们的收入增长并不能同步，当初的薪酬结构一直没有变化。此外，跳槽后的研发人员的薪酬是现在公司工资的一倍以上，当初行业中的高薪酬，现在已经开始跟不上外部公司的薪酬水平了。

问题：

1. 建业公司研发人员薪酬结构违背了哪些设计原则？（8分）

2. 薪酬组成结构模式有哪几种，你认为研发人员采用哪种薪酬组成结构模式比较合理？（12分）

第六篇　劳动关系管理

一、项目策划（1～2题，每题30分，共60分）

1. 背景资料

张明2009年3月入职深圳一电子公司，双方签订了一份为期3年的劳动合同，合同中特别约定：如违反公司规章制度，情节严重，公司有权提前解除劳动合同，且无须支付经济补偿金。2012年6月10日，张明接到公司的一份解雇通知，解雇理由是张明上班时间经常上网聊天，根据公司规章制度，3次以上在上班时间上网聊天则视为严重违纪，公司可解除劳动合同。张明辩解，他一直不知道公司有该规定，公司从未将规章制度的内容向其公示，公司称规章制度已向其公示，但无法举证规章制度公示的事实。

问题：

1. 请问公司可否就张明严重违纪的说法解除劳动合同？为什么？（15分）

2. 如何确定公司的规章制度合法有效？（15分）

2. 背景资料

2012 年 4 月 1 日，傅某加入上海一家软件公司，担任设计师工作，月薪 4000 元。2013 年 6 月开始担任公司首席设计师，月薪 9000 元。

2013 年 11 月 1 日傅某突然接到公司通知：公司将搬至北京，员工如果愿意随公司搬迁的，则继续留在公司工作；员工如果不愿随公司搬迁的，公司将于 11 月底解除劳动合同。

傅某不愿意随公司搬迁，于是公司于 2013 年 11 月底为傅某办理了退工手续，但补偿问题公司却拖延不决。傅某在多次与公司协商未果的情况下，申请了劳动仲裁。

问题：

1. 请问公司是否应该向傅某支付补偿金？为什么？（10 分）

2. 如果应该支付，那么补偿金的金额是多少？（10 分）

二、案例分析题（3~4 题，每题 20 分，共 40 分）

3. 背景资料

2010 年 1 月 10 日，小王入职时，公司告知他有 3 个月的试用期，但没有与小王签订书面的劳动合同。2010 年 3 月 15 日，公司通知小王，由于他在试用期表现不佳，所以公司决定辞退他。小王觉得很委屈，因为在试用期内他确实努力工作，而且自认为表现很好。

问题：

1. 请问公司的做法是否合法，为什么？（10 分）

2. 如果你是小王，你会怎么办？（10 分）

4. 背景资料

2009 年 2 月 1 日，甲公司与工会经过协商签订了集体合同，规定职工的月工资不低于 2000 元。2009 年 2 月 8 日，甲公司将集体合同文本送劳动行政部门审查，但劳动行政部门一直未予答复。2010 年 1 月，甲公司聘李某为销售经理，双方签订了为期 2 年的劳动合同，月工资 5000 元。几个月过去了，李某业绩不佳，公司渐渐对他失去了信心。2010 年 6 月，公司降低了李某的工资，只发给李某 1800 元工资。李某就此事与公司协商未果，因此申请了劳动争议仲裁。

问题：

1. 甲公司与工会签订的集体合同是否生效？为什么？（10 分）
2. 你认为仲裁机构会支持李某的请求吗？为什么？（10 分）

专业英语模拟试题

第一篇　专业英语模拟试卷 1

一、英汉互译（每题 2 分，共 30 分）

1. Apprenticeship

2. Career support

3. Outsourcing

4. Database

5. Employee empowerment

6. Goals

7. Human resource information system（HRIS）

8. Job rotation

9. Learning organization

10. Psychological contract

11. 薪资调查

12. 任务分析

13. 招募

14. 绩效管理

15. 工作丰富化

二、选词填空（每题 2 分，共 20 分）

A. feedback	B. benchmarking	C. rewards
D. Human resource management	E. benefit	F. on – the – job
G. performance	H. downsizing	I. Direct cost J. output

1. _____ refers to the practices and policies you need to carry out the people or personnel aspects of your management job.

2. Labor turnover rates provide a valuable means of _____ the effectiveness of HR policies and practices in organizations.

3. Labor turnover can be costly. _____ of recruiting and training replacements should be considered.

4. Business process re – engineering techniques are deployed as instruments for _____ .

5. Evaluations also fulfill the purpose of providing _____ to employees on how the organization views their performance.

6. The _____ of the job analysis should be a training or learning specification.

7. Coaching is a personal _____ technique designed to develop individual skills, knowledge, and attitudes.

8. Extrinsic _____ include direct compensation, indirect compensation, and nonfinancial rewards.

9. Flexible benefits allow employees to pick and choose from among a menu of

_____ options.

10. China's economic reformers have used material incentives in order to stimulate _____ .

三、单项选择题（每题 2 分，共 20 分）

1. The process of helping redundant employees to find other work or start new careers is _____ .

A. replacement

B. outplacement

C. release

D. downsizing

2. _____ focus the evaluator's attention on those behaviors that are key in making the difference between executing a job effectively or ineffectively.

A. The group order ranking

B. Written essay

C. The individual ranking

D. Critical incidents

3. The _____ plan should include plans for attracting good candidates by ensuring that the organization will become an "employer of choice".

A. outplacement

B. evaluation

C. recruitment

D. training

4. Organizational _____ and corporate plans indicate the direction in which the

organization is going.

A. goals

B. resource

C. result

D. process

5. _____ aims to broaden experience by moving people from job to job or department to department.

A. Job analysis

B. Job rotation

C. Job satisfaction

D. Job involvement

6. HR planning is _____ .

A. a technique that identifies the critical aspects of a job

B. the process of determining the human resources required by the organization to achieve its strategic goals

C. the process of setting major organizational objectives and developing comprehensive plans to achieve these objectives

D. the process of determining the primary direction of the firm

7. Career development programs benefit organizations in all of the following ways except _____ .

A. giving managers more control over their subordinates

B. giving managers increased skill in managing their own careers

C. providing greater retention of valued employees

D. giving an increased understanding of the organization

8. The area from which employers obtain certain types of workers is known as

the _____ .

A. labor market

B. region

C. recruiting area

D. supply region

9. A set of standards of acceptable conduct and moral judgment is known as

_____ .

A. morales

B. ethics

C. rules

D. legislation

10. Hiring someone outside the company to perform tasks that could be done internally is known as _____ .

A. outplacement

B. contracting

C. outsourcing

D. employee leasing

四、阅读理解（每题 3 分，共 30 分）

（一）

The context for obtaining the people required will be the labor markets in which the organization is operating which are:

（1）*The internal labor market* – the stocks and flows of people within the organization who can be promoted, trained, or re – deployed to meet future needs.

(2) *The external labor marker* – the external local, regional, national and international markets from which different sorts of people can be recruited. There are usually a number of markets, and the labor supply in these markets may vary considerably. Likely shortages will need to be identified so that steps can be taken to deal with them, for example by developing a more attractive "employment proposition".

As part of the human resource planning process, an organization may have to formulate "make or buy" policy decisions. A "make" policy means that organization prefers to recruit people at a junior level or as trainee, and rely mainly on promotion from within and training programs to meet future needs. A "buy" policy means that more reliance will be placed on recruiting from outside – "bringing fresh blood into the organization". In practice, organizations tend to mix the two choices together to varying degrees, depending on the situation of the firm and the type of people involves. A highly entrepreneurial company operating in the turbulent conditions, or one which has just started up, will probably rely almost entirely on external recruitment. When dealing with knowledge workers, there may be little choice—they tend to be much more mobile, and resourcing strategy may have to recognize that external recruitment will be the main source of supply. Management consultancies typically fall into this category. Firms which can predict people requirements fairly and accurately may rely more on developing their own staff once they have been recruited.

1. A "make" policy means that organization prefers to promote people from

_____.

A. regional labor market

B. national labor market

C. internal labor market

D. international labor market

2. According to the passge, management consultancies _____ .

A. are less mobile than people at a junior level

B. should be recruited from external labor market

C. should be promoted from within the organization

D. are not knowledge workers

3. If a firm can predict people requirements fairly accurately, it may

not _____ .

A. develop their own staff

B. formulate training programs

C. promote people from within the organization

D. rely more on recruiting from outside

4. "Make or buy" policy decision is a part of _____ .

A. human resource planning

B. training and development

C. performance appraisal

D. job analysis

5. the best title of this passage is _____ .

A. the organizational context of human resource planning

B. aims of human resource planning

C. the labor market context for human resource planning

D. limitations of human resource planning

(二)

Wlaters (1983) identifies nine sources of information which help to identify training priorities. These are：

（1）Organizational goals and corporate plans which indicate the direction in which the organization is going and, therefore, major training priorities.

（2）Human resource and succession planning which provides information on future skill requirements and management training needs.

（3）Personnel statistics on, for example, labor turnover, which highlight HR issues which might be addressed by training.

（4）Exit interviews which might suggest deficiencies in training arrangements.

（5）Consultation with senior managers which obtains opinions on training needs from key decision makers.

（6）Data on productivity, quality and performance which show where there are any gaps between expectations and results or negative trends, and therefore suggest training needs.

（7）Departmental layout changes which provide information about future developments and related training needs.

（8）Management requests for training which set out perceived needs.

（9）Knowledge of financial plans which determine whether the funds will be available for training, and may encourage fresh approaches if resources are limited.

Two other sources not directly mentioned by Walters are plans for introducing new technology or developing IT systems, and marketing plans which indicate where new skills are required to market new products or services, use different selling techniques or operate in new territories.

1. According to Wlaters, _____ is（are）major training priorities.

A. human resource and succession planning

B. personnel statistics

C. exit interviews

D. organizational goals and corporate plans

2. Human resource and succession planning provides information on _____ .

A. the direction in which the organization is going

B. future skill requirements and management training needs

C. deficiencies in training arrangements

D. any gaps between expectations and results or negative trends

3. The following sources of information which help to identify training priorities are mentioned by Wlaters except _____ .

A. marketing plans

B. departmental layout changes

C. data on productivity, quality and performance

D. consultation with senior managers

4. According to the passage, the following statements are true except _____ .

A. departmental layout changes provide information about future developments and related training needs

B. exit interviews highlight HR issues which might be addressed by training

C. data on productivity, quality and performance show where there are any gaps between expectations and results or negative trends

D. marketing plans indicate where new skills are required to market new products or services

5. The main topic about this passage is illustrating _____ .

A. sources of information which provide information on management training needs

B. sources of information of major training priorities

C. sources of information which help to identify training priorities

D. sources of information which provide information about future developments and related training needs

第二篇　专业英语模拟试卷 2

一、英汉互译（每题 2 分，共 30 分）

1. Centralization

2. Assessment center

3. Cultural shock

4. Expatriate

5. Hourly work

6. Internship programs

7. Job involvement

8. Management by objectives（MBO）

9. Pay – policy line

10. Self – appraisal

11. 360 度反馈

12. 甄选

13. 绩效评价

14. 工作规范

15. 间接成本

二、选词填空（每题 2 分，共 20 分）

A. promotion	B. job analysis	C. management
D. Globalization	E. job description	F. Human resource planning
G. competence	H. recruiting	I. mediation J. assessment

1. International human resource management includes _____ qualified personnel for overseas assignments.

2. Rapid _____ through an extensive staff ranking system is seen in one company as a very important motivational mechanism.

3. _____ refers to the tendency of firms to extend their sales or manufacturing to new markets abroad.

4. Developing a high – trust organization means creating trust between _____ and employees.

5. _____ determines the human resources required by the organization to achieve its strategic goals.

6. The _____ provides information on the nature and functions of the job.

7. The halo effect or error is the tendency for an evaluator to let the _____ of an individual on one trait influence his or her evaluation of that person on other traits.

8. Training is concerned with fitting people to take on extra responsibilities, increasing all – round _____ .

9. A training or a learning specification breaks down the broad duties contained in the _____ into the detailed tasks that must be carried out.

10. In case of labor disputes between the employer and laborers, the parties concerned can apply for _____ or arbitration, bring the case to courts, or settle them through consultation.

三、单项选择题（每题 2 分，共 20 分）

1. The placement of an employee in another job at a higher level in the organization with an increase in pay and status is known as a _____.

A. job enlargement

B. transfer

C. promotion

D. job rotation

2. Key jobs have all of the following characteristics except _____.

A. they are important to employees and the organization

B. they vary in terms of job requirements

C. they are used in salary surveys for wage determination

D. they are likely to vary in job content over time

3. A process that goes beyond TQM programs to a more comprehensive approach to process redesign is known as _____.

A. job redesign

B. process redesign

C. reengineering

D. rightsizing

4. The job specification describes job requirements relative to _____ .

A. skill and physical outputs

B. skill and physical demands

C. age and physical demands

D. experience and physical description

5. When determining where training emphasis should be placed, an examination of the goals, resources, and environment of the organization is known as _____ .

A. task analysis

B. organization analysis

C. resource analysis

D. skills analysis

6. The job evaluation system in which specific elements of the jobs to be evaluated are compared against similar elements of key jobs within the organization is known as _____ .

A. the point method

B. job ranking

C. the comparison method

D. the Hay profile method

7. The final decision to hire an applicant usually belongs to _____ .

A. the HR recruiter

B. the HR manager

C. line management

D. co – workers

8. Determining what the content of a training program should be, based on a study of the job duties, is known as _____ .

A. organization analysis

B. individual analysis

C. job analysis

D. task analysis

9. Sometimes organizations provide services to terminated employees that help them bridge the gap between their old position and a new job. These services are known as _____ .

A. downsizing programs

B. "headhunting" assistance programs

C. outplacement assistance

D. employee assistance programs（EAPs）

10. Job _____ form the basis for the administration of applicable employment tests.

A. outlines

B. specifications

C. requirements

D. details

四、阅读理解（每题 3 分，共 30 分）

（一）

Multiperson comparisons evaluate one individual's performance against one or more others. It is a relative rather than an absolute measuring device. The three most popular comparisons are group order ranking, individual ranking, and paired comparisons.

The group order ranking requires the evaluator to place employees into a particular classification, such as top one – fifth or second one – fifth. This method is often used in recommending students to graduate schools. Evaluators are asked to rank the student in the top five percent, the next five percent, the next fifteen percent, and so forth. But when used by managers to appraise employees, managers deal with all their subordinates. Therefore, if a rater has twenty subordinates, only four can be in the top fifth and, of course, four must also be relegated to the bottom fifth.

The individual ranking approach rank orders of employees from best to worst. If the manager is required to appraise thirty subordinates, this approach assumes that the difference between the first and second employee is the same as that between the twenty – first and twenty – second. Even though some of the employees may be closely grouped, this approach allows for no ties. The result is a clean ordering of employees, from the highest performer down to the lowest.

The paired comparison approach compares each employee with every other employee and rates each as either the superior or the weaker member of the pair. After all paired comparisons are made, each employee is assigned a summary ranking based on the number of superior scores he or she achieved. This approach ensures that each employee is compared against every other, but it can obviously become unwieldy when many employees are being compared.

Multiperson comparisons can be combined with one of the other methods to blend the best from both absolute and relative standards. For example, a college might use the graphic rating scale and the individual ranking method to provide more accurate information about its students' performance. The A, B, C, D, or E. A prospective employer or graduate school could then look at two students who each got a

"B" in their different financial accounting courses and draw considerably different conclusions about each where next to one grade it says "ranked fourth out of twenty – six", while the other says " ranked seventeenth out of thirty" . Obviously, the latter instructor gives out a lot more high grades!

1. Multiperson comparisons is a（an）_____ measuring device.

A. absolute

B. relative

C. accurate

D. false

2. According to the passage, there are three most popular comparisons except _____ .

A. group order ranking

B. individual ranking

C. graphic rating scales

D. paired comparisons

3. From this passage, we can infer that _____ .

A. recommending students to graduate schools often uses individual ranking

B. the paired comparison approach assumes that the difference between the first and second employee is same

C. group order ranking ensures that each employee is compared against every other

D. each method of multiperson comparisons can be used simultaneously

4. The following statements about individual ranking are false except _____ .

A. it rank orders of employees from the lowest performer up to the highest

B. the result is a clean ordering of employees

C. it assumes that the difference between the first and second employee is different

D. this approach allows for some of the employees who may be closely grouped

5. This article might be extracted from the paper about _____ .

A. performance appraisal

B. recruitment and replacement

C. training and development

D. reward systems

（二）

Our knowledge of motivation tells us that people do what they to satisfy needs. Before they do anything, they look for the payoff or reward. Many of these rewards – salary increases, employee benefits, preferred job assignments – are organizationally controlled.

The types of rewards that an organization can allocate are more complex than is generally thought. Obviously, there is direct compensation. But there are also indirect compensation and nonfinancial rewards. Each of these types of rewards can be distributed on an individual, group, or organization wide basis.

Intrinsic rewards are those that individuals receive for themselves. They are largely a result of the worker's satisfaction with his or her job. Techniques like job enrichment or any efforts to redesign or restructure work to increase personal worth to the employee may make his or her work more intrinsically rewarding.

Extrinsic rewards include direct compensation, indirect compensation, and nonfinancial rewards. Of course, an employee expects some forms of direct compensation: A basic wage or salary, overtime and holiday premium pay, bonuses based on performance, profit sharing, and/or possibly opportunities to purchase stock options. Employees will expect their direct compensation generally to align with their assessment of their contribution to the organization and, additionally, will expect it to be comparable to the direct compensation given to other employees with similar abilities and performance.

The organization will provide employees with indirect compensations: insurance, pay for holidays and vacations, services, and perquisites. In as much as these are generally made uniformly available to all employees at a given job level, regardless of performance, they are rally not motivating rewards. However, where indirect compensation is controllable by management and is used to reward performance, then it clearly needs to be considered as a motivating reward.

1. Rewards are often considered as a _____ function in human resource management.

A. planning

B. leading

C. motivating

D. controlling

2. Extrinsic rewards include the following except _____ .

A. job enrichment

B. direct compensation

C. indirect compensation

D. nonfinancial rewards

3. According to the passage, the following statements are false except _____ .

A. nonfinancial rewards belong to intrinsic rewards

B. overtime and holiday premium pay belongs to indirect compensation

C. employees will expect their direct compensation to be comparable to the indirect compensation given to other employees with similar abilities and performance

D. employees will expect their direct compensation generally to align with their assessment of their contribution to the organization

4. Perquisites which the organization provides employees belong to _____ .

A. intrinsic rewards

B. direct compensation

C. indirect compensation

D. nonfinancial rewards

5. The author of this passage would most likely agree that _____ .

A. if indirect compensation is controllable by management , then it can't be considered as a motivating reward

B. if indirect compensations are made uniformly available to all employees at a given job level, regardless of performance, they will lose their motivating function

C. techniques like job enrichment or nonfinancial rewards to increase personal worth to the employee may make his or her work more intrinsically rewarding

D. each type of rewards can be distributed on an individual or group, not organization wide basis

第三篇　专业英语模拟试卷 3

一、英汉互译（每题 2 分，共 30 分）

1. Bonus

2. Compensable factors

3. Delayering

4. Forecasting

5. Gain sharing plans

6. Job classification system

7. Minimum wage

8. Performance feedback

9. Staffing tables

10. Wage – rate compression

11. 培训

12. 即时奖金

13. 工资结构

14. 劳动力市场

15. 精简

二、选词填空（每题 2 分，共 20 分）

A. reward	B. job analysis	C. Human Resource management
D. ethics	E. benefit programs	F. human capital
G. agency	H. goals	I. contracts J. recruiting

1. For managers, the challenge of fostering intellectual or _____ lies in the fact that such Workers must be managed differently than were those of previous generations.

2. In summary, is _____ an integral part of every manager's job.

3. In the area of _____ and hiring, it's the line manager's responsibility to specify the qualifications employees need to fill specific positions.

4. HR manager also administers the various _____ (health and accident insurance, retirement, vacation, and so on).

5. Performance evaluations are used as the basis for _____ allocations.

6. Staff managers are authorized to assist and advise line managers in accomplishing these basic _____ .

7. Determining the nature of each employee's job is _____ .

8. Laborers shall fulfill their tasks of labor, improve their professional skills, follow rules on labor safety and sanitation, and observe labor discipline and professional _____ .

9. Labor _____ are agreements reached between laborers and the employer to

establish labor relationships and specify the rights, interests and obligations of each party.

10. In a public employment _____ , which served workers seeking employment and employers seeking workers, employment interviewers were appraised by the number of interviews they conducted.

三、单项选择题（每题 2 分，共 20 分）

1. The tendency for an evaluator to let the assessment of an individual on one trait influence his or her evaluation of that person on other traits is known as _____ .

A. similarity error

B. halo effect or error

C. leniency error

D. single criterion

2. The performance evaluation approach which compares each employee with every other employee and rates each as either the superior or the weaker member of the pair is known as _____ .

A. the paired comparison

B. the individual ranking

C. the group order ranking

D. critical incidents

3. Determining whether or not task performance is acceptable and studying the characteristics of individuals and groups that will be placed in the training environment are known as _____ .

A. person analysis

B. demographic analysis

C. individual analysis

D. group and individual analysis

4. The lines of advancement for an individual within an organization are known as _____ .

A. career paths

B. job progressions

C. career lines

D. job paths

5. Freedom from criterion deficiency of performance appraisals refers to the extent to which _____ .

A. standards relate to the overall objectives of the organization

B. standards capture the entire range of an employee's responsibilities

C. individuals tend to maintain a certain level of performance over time

D. factors outside the employee's control can influence performance

6. The Hay profile method uses which three factors for evaluating jobs? _____ .

A. Knowledge, skill, and responsibility

B. Mental ability, skill, and responsibility

C. Knowledge, mental ability, and responsibility

D. Knowledge, mental ability, and accountability

7. Which of the following is not an important component of a meaningful gain-sharing plan? _____ .

A. Establishing fair and precise measurement standards

B. Ensuring that bonus payout formulas are easy to calculate

C. Ensuring that bonus payouts are large enough to encourage future employee effort

D. Depending on top management to develop the gainsharing program

8. Giving employees more control over decisions about who their co – workers will be is known as _____ .

A. empowered selection

B. collaboration

C. team selection

D. group development

9. Which of the following is a technique used to elicit employee views in order to make decisions and initiate change? _____ .

A. Suggestion system

B. Downward communication

C. Attitude survey

D. Empowerment

10. Assessing the degree to which what employees learned during the training program is translated into enhanced employee performance is known as _____ .

A. results evaluation

B. reaction evaluation

C. behavior evaluation

D. learning evaluation

四、阅读理解（每题 3 分，共 30 分）

(一)

A training or a learning specification is a product of job analysis. It breaks down the broad duties contained in the job description into the detailed tasks that must be carried out. It then sets out the characteristics or attributes that the individual should have in order to perform these tasks successfully. These characteristics are:

• *Knowledge* – what the individual needs to know. It may be professional, technical or commercial knowledge. Or it may be about the commercial, economic, or market environment; the machines to be operated; the materials or equipment to be used or the procedures to be followed; or the customers, clients, colleagues and subordinates he or she is in contact with and the factors that affect their behavior. Or it may refer to the problems that occur and how they should be dealt with.

• *Skills* – what the individual needs to be able to do if results are to be achieved and knowledge is to be used effectively. Skills are built progressively by repeated training or other experience. They may be manual, intellectual or mental, perceptual or social.

• *Competences* – the behaviors' competences needed to achieve the levels of performance required.

• *Attitudes* – the disposition to behave or to perform in a way that is in accordance with the requirements of the work.

• *Performance standards* – what the fully competent individual has to be able to achieve.

1. A training or a learning specification is a product of _____ .

A. job structure

B. job evaluation

C. job design

D. job analysis

2. According to this passage, which of the following isn't the characteristic or at-

tribute that the individual should have in order to perform the task successfully? _____ .

A. Knowledge

B. Mental ability

C. Competences

D. Attitudes

3. According to this passage, the knowledge that the individual should have in order to perform the task successfully may include the following except _____ .

A. professional, technical or commercial knowledge

B. knowledge about the commercial, economic, or market environment

C. knowledge about the job description

D. the problems that occur and how they should be dealt with

4. From this passage, we can infer that _____ .

A. in order to perform tasks successfully, individuals need know more than their professional knowledge

B. in order to perform tasks successfully, skills that the individual should have are built only by repeated training

C. in order to perform tasks successfully, the disposition to behave or to perform in a way needn't be in accordance with the requirements of the work

D. in order to perform tasks successfully, performance standards should be based on what the average individual has to be able to achieve

5. The best title of this passage is _____ .

A. job analysis

B. training or learning specification

C. job description

D. performance standards

（二）

Supply forecasting measures the number of people likely to be available from within and outside the organization, having allowed for attrition, absenteeism, internal movements and promotions, and changes in hours and other conditions of work. The forecast will be based on:

• An analysis of existing human resources in terms of numbers in each occupation, skills and potentials;

• Forecast losses to existing resources through attrition (the analysis of labor wastage is an important aspect of human resource planning, because it provides the basis for plans to improve retention rates);

• Forecast changes to existing resources through internal promotions;

• The effect of changing conditions of work and absenteeism;

• Sources of supply from within the organization;

• Sources of supply from outside the organization in the national and local labor markets.

Mathematical modeling techniques aided by computers can help in the preparation of supply forecasts in situations where comprehensive and reliable data on stocks and flows be provided. As this is rarely the case, they are seldom used.

The demand and supply forecasts can then be analyzed to determine whether there are any deficits or surplus. This provides the basis for recruitment, retention and, if unavoidable, downsizing plans. Computerized planning models can be used for this purpose. It is, however, not essential to rely on a software planning package. The basic forecasting calculations can be carried out with a spreadsheet which, for each occupation where plans need to be made, sets out and calculates the number required as in the following example:

(1) Number currently employed   70

(2) Annual wastage rate based on past records   10%

(3) Expected losses during the year   7

(4) Balance at end – year   63

(5) Number required at end – year   75

(6) Number to be obtained during year (= 5 − 4)   8

1. The word "attrition" in the first paragraph means _____ .

A. retention rates

B. supply from within the organization

C. supply from outside the organization

D. labor wastage and retirements

2. According to the passage, forcasting the future supply of people should be based on the following except _____ .

A. forecast losses to existing resources through attrition

B. forecast changes to existing resources through external movements

C. the effect of changing conditions of work

D. sources of supply from external labor markets

3. The author of this passage might disagree that _____ .

A. the demand and supply forecasts can be analyzed to determine whether there are any deficits or surplus

B. the demand and supply forecasts can provide the basis for recruitment, retention

C. the demand and supply forecasts can't provide the basis for downsizing

D. a spreadsheet can be used for demand and supply forecasting

4. In a company, if people currently employed are 300, annual wastage rate is 20%, and number required at end – year is 350, then the company should recruit _____ .

A. 100

B. 110

C. 120

D. 130

5. This passage may be extracted from the paper about _____ .

A. human resource planning

B. training and development

C. recruitment and replacement

D. international human resource management

第四篇 专业英语模拟试卷 4

一、英汉互译（每题 2 分，共 30 分）

1. Work permit

2. Strategic congruence

3. Return on investment（ROI）

4. Personnel selection

5. Peer appraisal

6. Mediation

7. Job satisfaction

8. Downward move

9. Database

10. Critical incident method

11. 行动计划

12. 职业

13. 员工授权

14. 人力资源信息系统

15. 关键工作

二、选词填空（每题 2 分，共 20 分）

A. competition	B. arbitration	C. external labor markets
D. careers	E. outplacement	F. job description
G. forecasting	H. expatriate	I. halo effect J. skills

1. The analysis of the number of people leaving the organization (labor turnover of wastage) provides data for use in supply _____.

2. Demand forecasting is the process of estimating the future numbers of people required and the likely _____ and competences they will need.

3. The _____ are the external local, regional, national and international markets from which different sorts of people can be recruited.

4. From tapping the global labor force to formulating selection, training, and compensation policies for _____ employees managing globalization will thus be a major HR challenge in the next few years.

5. The pressure for improved performance to meet more intense global _____ explains why many organizations are seeing higher standards for employees.

6. People also leave organizations voluntarily to further their _____, get more money or move away from the district.

7. Organizational release activities deal with redundancy, _____, dismissal, voluntary turnover and retirement.

8. Once a labor dispute occurs, the party that has objections to the ruling of the

labor _____ committee can bring the case to a peoples court.

9. A training or a learning specification breaks down the broad duties contained in the _____ into the detailed tasks that must be carried out.

10. The _____ is the tendency for an evaluator to let the assessment of an individual on one trait influence his or her evaluation of that person on other traits.

三、单项选择题（每题 2 分，共 20 分）

1. Eliminating what are deemed to be unnecessary layers of management and supervision is known as _____ .

A. delayering

B. downsizing

C. right – sizing

D. benchmarking

2. The changing environments of Human Resource Management include the following except _____ .

A. work force diversity

B. technological trends

C. globalization

D. great changes in the nature of work force

3. The aims of human resource planning in any organization might be the following except _____ .

A. attract and retain the number of people required with the appropriate skills, expertise and competences

B. reduce dependence on external recruitment when key skills are in short supply by formulating retention, as well as employee development, strategies

C. neglect the problems of potential surpluses or deficits of people

D. develop a well – trained and flexible workforce, thus contributing to the organization's ability to adapt to an uncertain and changing environment

4. Forcasting the supply of people should be based on the following except _____.

A. forecast losses to existing resources through attrition

B. recruitment plans

C. the effect of changing conditions of work

D. sources of supply from external labor markets

5. The costs of labor turnover include the following except _____.

A. direct cost of recruiting replacements

B. opportunity cost of time spent by HR and line managers in recruitment

C. loss arising from reduced input from new starters until they are fully trained

D. indirect cost of training replacements in the unnecessary skills

6. Assessing the sets of skills and knowledge employees need to be successful, particularly for decision – oriented and knowledge – intensive jobs, is known as _____.

A. individual assessment

B. competency assessment

C. organizational assessment

D. job assessment

7. Which system of job evaluation is being used when jobs are classified according to a series of predetermined wage grades? _____.

A. Hay profile method

B. Job ranking

C. Factor comparison method

D. Job classification system

8. The purpose of a profit – sharing plan is to _____ .

A. allow workers to contribute specific knowledge to improving the organization

B. motivate a total commitment to the organization as a whole

C. enable workers to share in labor cost savings

D. instill commitment to the employees' immediate work group

9. One of the primary benefits of cross – training employees is that _____ .

A. cross – training enables individuals to exert more effort on their job

B. cross – training helps employees identify trouble spots that cut across several jobs

C. cross – training enables managers to spend less time supervising individual performance

D. cross – training enables managers to save more money in labor costs

10. Which of the following is not an approach used by organizations to try to lower labor costs? _____ .

A. Downsizing

B. Outsourcing

C. Productivity enhancements

D. Employee development

四、阅读理解（每题 3 分，共 30 分）

（一）

Although the notion of human resource planning is well established in the HRM vocabulary, it does not seem to be commonly practiced as a key HR activity. As Rothwell (1995) suggests, "apart from isolated examples, there has been little research evidence of increased use or of its success". She explains the gap between theory and practice as arising from:

- The impact of change and the difficulty of predicting the future – "the need for planning may be in inverse proportion to its feasibility";

- The "shifting kaleidoscope" of policy priorities and strategies within organizations;

- The distrust displayed by many managers of theory or planning – they often prefer pragmatic adaptation to conceptualization;

- The lack of evidence that human resource planning works.

Be that as it may, it is difficult to reject out of hand the belief that some attempt should be made broadly to forecast future human resource requirements as a basis for planning and action. On the basis of research conducted by the Institute for Employment Studies, Reilly (1999) has suggested a number of reasons why organizations choose to engage in some forms of human resource planning. These fall into the following three groups.

（1）Planning for substantive reasons, that is, to have a practical effect by optimizing the use of resources and / or making them more flexible, acquiring and nurturing skills that take time to develop, identifying potential problems and minimizing the chances of making a bad decision.

（2）Planning because of the process benefits, which involves understanding the present in order to confront the future, challenging assumptions and liberating thinking, making explicit decisions which can later be challenged, standing back and providing an overview, and ensuring that long – term thinking is not driven out by short – term focus.

（3）Planning for organizational reasons, which involves communicating plans so as to obtain support / adherence to them, linking HR plans to business plans so as to influence them, regaining corporate control over operating units, and coordinating and integrating organizational decision – making and actions.

1. According Rothwell（1995）, the gap between human resource planning theory and practice arised from the following except _____ .

A. the impact of change and the difficulty of predicting the future

B. the dramatic change of policy priorities and strategies within organizations

C. the distrust displayed by many managers of theory or planning

D. the redundance of evidence that human resource planning works

2. According to the passage, which of the following statements is true? _____ .

A. The definition of human resource planning is not well established

B. Rothwell（1995）suggests there has been no example of success about human resource planning

C. Human resource planning does not seem to be commonly practiced as a key HR activity

D. The gap between human resource planning theory and practice is very small

3. Reilly (1999) has suggested a number of reasons why organizations choose to engage in some forms of human resource planning, but which of the following is not included? _____ .

A. Planning has a theoritical effect by optimizing the use of resources

B. Planning can be used to identify potential problems and minimize the chances of making a bad decision

C. Planning involves understanding the present in order to confront the future

D. Planning for organizational reasons

4. About the human resource planning process benefits, the author of this passage might disagree that _____ .

A. it can challenge assumptions

B. it can minimize the chances of making a bad decision

C. it can liberate thinking

D. it can ensuring that long – term thinking is not driven out by short – term focus

5. From this passage, we can infer that _____ .

A. we should forecast future human resource requirements as a basis for planning and action

B. there is no evidence that human resource planning works

C. there is no use for human resource planning

D. there is no organizational reasons for human resource planning

（二）

The criteria or criterion that management chooses to evaluate, when appraising employee performance, will have a major influence on what employees do. The three most popular sets of criteria are individual task outcomes, behaviors, and traits.

If ends count, rather than means, then management should evaluate an employee's task outcomes. Using task outcomes, a plant manager could be judged on criteria such as quantity produced, scrap generated, and cost per unit of production. Similarly, a salesperson could be assessed on overall sales volume in his or her territory, dollar increase in sales, and number of new accounts established.

In many cases, it's difficult to identify specific outcomes that can be directly attributable to an employee's actions. This is particularly true of personnel in staff positions and individuals whose work assignments are intrinsically part of a group effort. In the latter case, the group's performance may be readily evaluated, but the contribution of each group member may be difficult or impossible to identify clearly. In such instances, it is not unusual for management to evaluate the employee's behavior. Using the previous examples, behaviors of a plant manager that could be used for performance evaluation purpose might include promptness in submitting his or her monthly reports or the leadership style that the manager exhibits. Pertinent salesperson behaviors could be average number of contact calls made per day or sick days used per year.

The weakest set of criteria, yet one that is still widely used by organizations, is individual traits. We say they are weaker than either task outcomes or behaviors because they are farthest removed from the actual performance of the job itself. Traits such as having "a good attitude," showing "confidence," being "intelligent" or "friendly", "looking busy", or possessing "a wealth of experience" may or may not be highly correlated with positive task outcomes, but only the naive would ignore the reality that such traits are frequently used in organizations as criteria for assessing an employee's level of performance.

1. According to the passage, which of the following is not the criteria that man-

agement chooses to evaluate employees' performance? _____ .

A. Individual task outcomes

B. Individual behaviors

C. Individual skills

D. Individual traits

2. Criteria of task outcomes which can be used for a plant manager include the following except _____ .

A. quantity produced

B. dollar increase in sales

C. scrap generated

D. cost per unit of production

3. Behaviors of salesperson that could be used for performance evaluation purpose might include _____ .

A. promptness in submitting his or her monthly reports

B. the leadership style that the manager exhibits

C. number of new accounts established

D. average number of contact calls made per day

4. Traits that could be used for performance evaluation purpose might include the following except _____ .

A. having "a good apperance"

B. showing "confidence"

C. being "intelligent" or "friendly"

D. possessing "a wealth of experience"

5. The author of this passage might most likely agree that _____ .

A. the criteria or criterion that management evaluate employees' performance will have a minor influence on what employees do

B. if means count, rather than ends, then management should evaluate an employee's task outcomes

C. the contribution of individuals whose work assignments are intrinsically part of a group effort can be easy to identify clearly

D. individual traits is the weakest set of criteria that can be used for performance evaluation

第五篇　专业英语模拟试卷 5

一、英汉互译（每题 2 分，共 30 分）

1. Assessment center

2. Bonus

3. Development planning system

4. Expert systems

5. Human capital

6. Intraorganizational bargaining

7. Job evaluation

8. Organizational analysis

9. Peer appraisal

10. Wage and salary survey

11. 自我评估

12. 产出

13. 工作结构

14. 计时工资制

15. 集权化

二、选词填空（每题 2 分，共 20 分）

A. job satisfaction	B. recruiting	C. organizational learning	
D. pay systems	E. strategic plan	F. wage levels	
G. motivational	H. needs	I. performance	J. productive

1. In the management of international joint ventures, Pucik（1988）argues that one of the main challenges anywhere is the _____ capacity of the partners within the joint venture.

2. Rapid promotion through an extensive staff ranking system is seen in one company as a very important _____ mechanism.

3. Generally money is seen as important for _____ and retaining employees, but not as a real motivator.

4. China's economic reformers have used material incentives in order to stimulate _____ .

5. New labor laws permit companies to set their own _____ .

6. Organizations are finding that IHRM activities are best handled by linking them to the enterprise's _____ .

7. An extensive review of the literature indicates that the more important factors conducive to _____ include mentally challenging work, equitable rewards, supportive working conditions, and supportive colleagues.

8. Employees want _____ and promotion policies that they perceive as being

just, unambiguous, and in line with their expectations.

9. The early views on the satisfaction – performance relationship can be essentially summarized in the statement "a happy worker is a _____ worker" .

10. Giving all employees the same benefits assumes all employees have the same _____ .

三、单项选择题（每题 2 分，共 20 分）

1. An interview in which an applicant is given a hypothetical incident and is asked how he or she would respond to it is a _____ .

A. computer interview

B. panel interview

C. situational interview

D. nondirective interview

2. The desired outcomes of training programs are formally stated as _____ .

A. training goals

B. learning objectives

C. instructional objectives

D. learning goals

3. Career counseling involves talking with employees about all of the following except _____ .

A. their current job activities and performance

B. their past career decisions

C. their personal and career interests and goals

D. their personal skills

4. In most instances, who is in the best position to perform the function of appraising an employee's performance? _____ .

A. Someone from the HR department

B. The employee's supervisor

C. The employee

D. Co – workers

5. The process of determining the relative worth of jobs in order to determine pay rates for different jobs is known as _____ .

A. job determination

B. job diagnosis

C. job analysis

D. job evaluation

6. Profit sharing refers to any procedure by which an employer pays employees _____ .

A. an incentive based on their merit

B. an incentive based on labor cost savings

C. a bonus based on the overall productivity of their particular work group

D. current or deferred sums based on the organization's financial performance

7. All of the following are prevalent reasons for failure among expatriates except _____ .

A. a spouse's inability to adapt

B. a manager's personality

C. inability to cope with larger responsibilities

D. distaste for travel

8. Communication systems should provide accurate information regarding all of

the following except _____ .

A. business plans and goals

B. employee background and personal data

C. unit and corporate operating results

D. incipient problems and opportunities

9. Reengineering often requires that managers start from scratch in rethinking all of the following except _____ .

A. how work should be done

B. how technology and people should interact

C. how the entire organization should be structured

D. how organizations should compete

10. The core job dimension that describes the degree to which a job has a substantial impact on the lives or work of other people is called _____ .

A. skill variety

B. task identity

C. task significance

D. autonomy

四、阅读理解（每题 3 分，共 30 分）

（一）

Human resource planning, in the broader meaning of the term, is one of the fundamental strategic roles of the HR function. HR can make a major contribution to developing the resource capability of the firm and therefore its strategic capability by systematically reviewing the firm's strategic objectives and by ensuring that plans are made that will ensure that the human resources are available to meet those objectives. Thus HR is focusing on the acquisition and development of the human capital required by the organization.

To make this contribution, heads of HR and their colleagues in the HR function need to:

 • Ensure that they are aware of the strategic plans of the business and can provide advice on the human resource implications of those plans;

 • Point out to management the strengths and weakenesses of the human resources of the organization, and the opportunities and treats they present, so that these can be considered when developing business plans;

 • Be capable of scenario planning in the sense that they can identify future issues concerning the acquisition, retention and employment of people and advise on methods of addressing those issues;

 • Understand the extent to which quantitative assessments of the future demand for and supply of people may be feasible and useful, and know the methods that can be used to prepare such forecasts;

 • Understand how to analyze the cost of labor turnover and to establish reasons for leaving;

 • Be aware of the scope to deal with future requirements by introducing various forms of flexibility;

 • Be capable of preparing relevant and practical resourcing plans and strategies for retaining people, based upon an understanding of the internal and external environment of the organization and the implications of analyses of labor turnover.

 1. In the broader meaning of the term, human resource planning plays a (an)

_____ in the HR function.

A. strategic role

B. tactical role

C. objective role

D. no role

2. Which of the following measures isn't the one by which HR can make a major contribution to developing the resource capability of the firm and its strategic capability? _____ .

A. By systematically examining the firm's strategic objectives

B. By ensuring that plans will ensure the available human resources to meet the firm's strategic objectives

C. By focusing on the acquisition and development of the people required by the organization

D. By focusing on firing and outplacing the redunant employees

3. To make a major contribution to developing the resource capability of the firm and its strategic capability, staff of HR need to do the following except _____ .

A. ensure that they learn the strategic plans of the business

B. point out to management the advantages and disadvantages of the human resources of the organization

C. be aware of the scope to deal with existing requirements by introducing various forms of flexibility

D. be capable of preparing relevant and practical resourcing plans and strategies for retaining people

4. From the passage, we can't infer that _____ .

A. human resource planning is one of the HR function

B. HR can make a major contribution to developing the resource capability of the firm and therefore its strategic capability without HR planning

C. it is the task of all staff of HR to develop the resource capability of the firm and therefore its strategic capability

D. to develop the resource capability of the firm and therefore its strategic capability, HR must be focus on the acquisition and development of the human capital required by the organization

5. The main topic of this passage is _____ .

A. the contribution of HR to human resource planning

B. the contribution of human resource planning to HR

C. the contribution of HR

D. the contribution of human resource planning

（二）

Job rotation aims to broaden experience by moving people from job to job or department to department. It can be an inefficient and frustrating method of acquiring additional knowledge and skills unless it is carefully planned and controlled. What has sometimes been referred to as the "Cook's tour" method of moving trainees (usually management trainees) from department to department has incurred much justified criticism because of the time wasted by trainees in departments where no one knew what to do with them or cared.

It may be better to use the term "planned sequence of experience" rather than "job rotation" to emphasize that the experience should be programmed to satisfy a training specification for acquiring knowledge and skills in different departments and occupations. It can be argued in support of job rotation that if it is by experience that adults learn, then that experience should be planned.

Success in using this method depends on designing a program that sets down what the trainee is expected to learn in each department or job in which he or she gains experience. There must also be a suitable person available to see that the trainee is given the right experience or opportunity to learn, and arrangements must be made to check progress. For apprentices this will mean the use of training supervisors within departments to see that the training syllabus is followed, and the use of logbooks to record what experience has been gained. The syllabus within a department should include specific assignments or projects. A good way of stimulating trainees to find out for themselves is to provide them with a list of questions to answer; it is essential however, to follow up each segment of experience to check what has been learned and, if necessary, modify the program.

1. What is the main aim of job rotation? _____ .

A. Acquire basic knowledge

B. Broaden experience

C. Acquire basic skills

D. Move people from job to job

2. If employers want to broaden employees' experience through job rotation, they must _____ .

A. plan and controll job rotation

B. move people from department to department

C. move people from job to job

D. plan and controll the recruitment of employees

3. If we want to make success in using job rotation, we should do the following things except _____ .

A. design a program that sets down what the trainee is expected to learn in each department or job

B. ensure a suitable person available to see that the trainee is given the right experience or opportunity to learn

C. make arrangements to check progress

D. provide the trainee with no question to answer

4. From this passage, we can't conclude that _____ .

A. job rotation has never incurred any criticism

B. the aim of using the term "planned sequence of experience" is to emphasize that the experience should be programmed to satisfy a training specification

C. if it is by experience that adults learn, then that experience should be planned

D. a good way of stimulating trainees to find out for themselves is to provide them with a list of questions to answer

5. This passage might be extracted from the paper about _____ .

A. HR planning techniques

B. selecting techniques

C. training techniques

D. motivating techniques

第六篇 专业英语模拟试卷 6

一、英汉互译（每题 2 分，共 30 分）

1. Apprenticeship

2. Career management system

3. Cross – training

4. Differential piece rate

5. Employee leasing

6. Human resources planning

7. Job enrichment

8. Management by objectives（MBO）

9. Outsourcing

10. Reengineering

11. 技能工资

12. 利润分享

13. 工作轮换

14. 投入

15. 数据库

二、选词填空（每题2分，共20分）

A. assessment	B. benefits	C. job analysis
D. critical incident	E. human capital	F. recruitment
G. selection	H. on – the – job	I. forecasts J. costs

1. The ＿＿＿＿ provides information on the nature and functions of the job.

2. HR is focusing on the acquisition and development of the ＿＿＿＿ required by the organization.

3. The downsizing plan should be based on the timing of reductions and of ＿＿＿＿ the extent to which these can be achieved by natural wastage or voluntary redundancy.

4. Rapid turnover can result simply from poor ＿＿＿＿ or promotion decisions.

5. A flexibility plan can contain proposals to reduce overtime ＿＿＿＿ through the use of flexible hours.

6. Job – sharing is an arrangement where by two employees share the work of one full – time position, dividing pay and ＿＿＿＿ between them according to the time each works.

7. The ＿＿＿＿ plan should include plans for attracting good candidates by ensuring that the organization will become an "employer of choice".

8. Behaviorally anchored rating scales combine major elements from the ＿＿＿＿ and graphic rating scale approaches.

9. 360 – degree feedback is also referred to as multi – source _____ or multi –
rater feedback.

10. Coaching is a personal _____ technique designed to develop individual
skills, knowledge, and attitudes.

三、单项选择题（每题 2 分，共 20 分）

1. Questions contained in structured job interviews should be based on _____.

A. job analysis

B. job design

C. job specialization

D. job utilization

2. A process in which individuals are evaluated as they participate in a series of
situations that resemble what they might be called upon to handle on the job is known
as a/an _____.

A. management training seminar

B. executive development program

C. in – basket exercise

D. assessment center

3. If your primary objective for a performance appraisal is to give employees developmental feedback, which of the following appraisal methods should you use?
_____.

A. Trait method

B. Results method

C. Behavior method

D. Attitudinal method

4. Outplacement services are _____ .

A. useful methods of attracting individuals into a career

B. designed to help terminated employees find a job elsewhere

C. rarely given to executive employees

D. vital parts of any career management system

5. Transnational teams tend to be _____ .

A. focused on projects that span multiple countries

B. comprised of members with generalized skills

C. homogenous

D. comprised of members from the same region

6. Which of the following compensation systems does not focus employee efforts on outcomes that are beneficial to both themselves and the organization as a whole? _____ .

A. Profit – sharing plans

B. Employee stock ownership plans

C. Hourly based pay systems

D. Skill – based pay systems

7. The total – quality HR paradigm would likely emphasize all of the following except _____ .

A. cross – functional training

B. team/group – based rewards

C. autocratic leadership

D. customer and peer performance reviews

8. A group of employees rotating jobs as they complete the production or service

process is called a/an _____ .

A. labor bargaining unit

B. employee team

C. training – production group

D. employee rotation unit

9. Notifying applicants of the selection decision and making job offers are generally the responsibility of _____ .

A. the HR department

B. the line manager

C. the supervisor

D. the industrial relations manager

10. Performance appraisals are used most widely as a basis for _____ .

A. determining training needs

B. discharging decisions

C. deciding compensation

D. directing performance improvement

四、阅读理解（每题3分，共30分）

（一）

The labor turnover index (sometimes referred to as employee or labor wastage index) is the traditional formula for measuring wastage. It has been described by the CIPD as the "crude wastage method". It is calculated as follows:

$$\frac{\text{Number of leavers in a specified period (usually 1 year)}}{\text{Average number of employees during the same period}} \times 100$$

This method is commonly used because it is easy to calculate and to understand. For human resource planning purposes, it is a simple matter to work out that if a company wanted to increase its workforce by 50 people from 150 to 200 but the labor turnover rate is 20 percent (a loss of 30 people), then if this trend continues, the company would have to recruit 90 employees during the following year in order to increase and to hold the workforce at 200 in that year (50 extra employees, plus 40 to replace the 20 percent wastage of the average 200 employees employed). It can also be used to make comparisons with other organizations that will typically adopt this method.

This wastage formula may be simple to use but it can be misleading. The main objection to the measurement of turnover in terms of the proportion of those who leave in given period is that the figure may be inflated by the high turnover of a relatively small proportion of the workforce, especially in times of heavy recruitment. Thus, a company employing 150 people might have had an annual wastage rate of 20 percent, meaning that 30 jobs had become vacant during the year. But this could have been spread throughout the company, covering all occupations and long – as well as short – service employees. Alternatively, it could have been restricted to a small sector of the workforce – only 20 jobs might have been affected although each of these had to be filled 10 times during the year. These are totally different situations, and unless they are understood, inaccurate forecasts would be made of future requirements and inappropriate actions would b taken to deal with the problem. The turnover index is also suspect if the average number of employees upon which the percentage is based is unrepresentative of recent trends because of considerable increases or decreases during the period in the numbers employed.

1. The aim of the labor turnover index is to _____ .

A. measure labor turnover

B. analyze the reasons of labor turnover

C. measure costs of labor turnover

D. analyze the significance of labor turnover

2. If a company has 500 people and its labor turnover rate is 20 percent in a specified period, the labor turnover index of the company is _____.

A. 0.2

B. 2

C. 20

D. 200

3. If a company want to increase its workforce from 400 to 500 but the labor turnover rate is 10 percent (a loss of 40 people), then if this trend continues, the company has to recruit _____ employees during the following year.

A. 100

B. 140

C. 150

D. 200

4. Which of the following isn't the reason that the labor turnover index can be misleading? _____.

A. The figure may be inflated by the high turnover

B. The labor turnover rate of every occupation may be different

C. The average number of employees upon which the percentage is based is un-representative of recent trends

D. The labor turnover index is too simple

5. According to the passage, the author might most likely disagree that _____.

A. the labor turnover index is an traditional method for measuring labor turnover

B. the labor turnover index is commonly used because the calculation is accurate

C. the labor turnover index can be compared with the one of other organizations

D. the labor turnover index can be criticized

(二)

There are three basic types of employment agencies: (a) those operated by federal, state, or local governments; (b) those associated with nonprofit organizations; and (c) privately owned agencies.

Public state employment service agencies exist in every state. They are aided and coordinated by the U. S. Department of Labor, which also maintains a nationwide computerized job bank to which all state employment offices are connected. Using the computer – listed job information, an agency interviewer is better able to counsel job applicants concerning available jobs in their local and other geographical areas.

Although public agencies are a major source of blue – collar and white – collar workers, the experience of some employers with these agencies has been mixed. Applicants for unemployment insurance are required to register with these agencies. They must make themselves available for job interviews to collect their unemployment payments. A fraction of these people are not interested in getting back to work, so employers can end up with applicants who have little or no real desire to obtain immediate employment.

Other employment agencies are associated with nonprofit organizations. For example, most professional and technical societies have units that help their members find jobs. Similarly, many public welfare agencies try to place people who are in special categories, such as those who are physically disabled or are war veterans.

Private employment agencies are important sources of clerical, white – collar, and managerial personnel. Such agencies charge fees for each applicant they place. These fees are usually set by state law and are posted in their offices. Whether the employer or the candidate pays the fee is mostly determined by market conditions. However, the trend has been toward "fee – paid jobs" in which the employer pays the fees. The assumption is that the most qualified candidates are presently employed and would not be as willing to switch jobs if they had to pay the fees themselves. Many private agencies now offer temporary help service and provide secretarial, clerical, or semiskilled labor on a short term basis. These agencies can be useful in helping you cope with peak loads and fill in for vacationing employees.

1. The basic types of employment agencies include the following except _____.

A. employment agencies operated by federal, state, or local governments

B. employment agencies associated with nonprofit organizations

C. employment agencies privately owned

D. employment agencies owned by the U. S. Department of Labor

2. Which of the following statements about public agencies is false? _____.

A. They exist in every state

B. They are coordinated by the U. S. Department of Labor

C. They are a major source of blue – collar and managerial personnel

D. They are connected by a nationwide computerized job bank

3. About applicants for unemployment insurance, the author might most likely agree that _____.

A. they must register with all employment agencies

B. they must make themselves available for job interviews to collect their unem-

254

ployment payments

C. none of these people are not interested in getting back to work

D. employers can't end up with applicants who have little or no real desire to obtain immediate employment

4. According to the passage, which of the following on private employment agencies can't be concluded? _____ .

A. They are important sources of knowledge workers

B. Fees that they charge for each applicant they place are usually in line with state law

C. Market conditions determine who pay the fees

D. No private agencies will offer temporary help service and provide secretarial, clerical, or semiskilled labor on a short term basis

5. This passage might be extracted from the paper about _____ .

A. recruitment

B. selection

C. training

D. performance evaluation

第七篇　专业英语模拟试卷 7

一、英汉互译（每题 2 分，共 30 分）

1. Behavior modeling

2. Compensable factors

3. Electronic performance support system（EPSS）

4. Feedback

5. Internship programs

6. Job classification system

7. Mediation

8. On‐the‐job training（OJT）

9. Peer appraisal

10. Psychological contract

11. 培训

12. 津贴

13. 工作结构

14. 计时工资制

15. 职业支持

二、选词填空（每题 2 分，共 20 分）

A. careers	B. arbitration	C. pay levels
D. apprenticeship	E. employment agencies	F. alternative
G. benefit package	H. recruiting	I. contract J. training

1. The quality of a firm's _____ process had a big impact on what candidates thought of the firm.

2. Private _____ are important sources of clerical, white – collar, and managerial personnel.

3. At Xerox, unionized hourly workers over 55 with 15 years of service and those over 50 with 20 years of service can bid on jobs at lower stress and lower _____ if they desire so.

4. People also leave organizations voluntarily to further their _____, get more money or move away from the district.

5. Outplacement is about helping redundant employees to find _____ work.

6. Three types of third – party interventions are used to overcome an impasse: mediation, fact – finding, and _____ .

7. Approximately half of the German youth between the ages of 15 – 18 are enrolled in _____ programs.

8. Terms of employment tend to be very technical and are governed by a _____ that spells out exactly what each side will do for the other.

9. Salary and _____ tend to be secret, so no one knows what anyone else is receiving.

10. Every year the company selects dozens of junior managers and young employees to attend universities in order to undertake _____ programs, even degree courses.

三、单项选择题（每题 2 分，共 20 分）

1. All of the following are basic skills needed for successful career management except _____ .

A. developing a positive attitude

B. establishing goals

C. adopting the mindset of your superiors

D. putting responsibility for your career in the hands of your supervisor

2. Which training method focuses upon learning at the affective level? _____ .

A. Sensitivity training

B. Apprenticeship training

C. Intercultural motivation

D. Multilingual training

3. A total – quality paradigm tends to emphasize which of the following facets of organizational training efforts? _____ .

A. Job – related skills

B. Cross – functional skills

C. Functional, technical skills

D. A narrow range of skills

4. Performance appraisal methods can be broadly classified as either _____, _____, or _____ approaches.

A. trait, behavioral, judgmental

B. trait, behavioral, results

C. behavioral, judgmental, results

D. behavioral, judgmental, attitudinal

5. When managers talk about "going global" they have to balance a complicated set of issues that include all of the following except _____ .

A. geographical differences

B. cultural differences

C. legal differences

D. personal differences

6. The selection procedure usually begins with _____ .

A. employment tests

B. a medical examination

C. a supervisory interview

D. completion of an application form

7. It is recommended that a diagnosis of poor employee performance focus on all of the following except _____ .

A. skill

B. personality

C. effort

D. external conditions

8. When employees receive a higher rate of pay for all of their work if production exceeds a standard level of output, under which incentive plan are they working?

_____ .

A. Differential piece rate

B. Standard piece rate

C. Exception bonus rate

D. Individual rate pay

9. Cultural environment includes all of the following except _____ .

A. education/human capital

B. values/ideologies

C. corporate structure

D. religious beliefs

10. Conducting job analysis is usually the primary responsibility of the _____ .

A. job incumbent

B. line supervisors

C. accounting department

D. HR department

四、阅读理解（每题 3 分，共 30 分）

（一）

Many promotable candidates are originally hired through college recruiting. This is therefore an important source of management trainees, as well as of professional and technical employees.

There are two main problems with on – campus recruiting. First, it is relatively expensive and time – consuming for the recruiters. Schedules must be set well in advance, company brochures printed, records of interviews kept, and much recruiting time spent on campus. Second, recruiters themselves are sometimes ineffective, or worse. Some recruiters are unprepared, show little interest in the candidate, and act superior. Many recruiters also don't effectively screen their student candidates. For example, students' physical attractiveness often outweighs other more valid traits and skills. Some recruiters also tend to assign females to "female – type" jobs and males to "male – type" jobs. Such findings underscore the need to train recruiters before sending them to the campus.

You have two goals as a campus recruiter. Your main function is screening, which means determining whether a candidate is worthy of further consideration. Exactly which traits you look for will depend on your specific recruiting needs. Traits to assess include motivation, communication skills, education, appearance, and attitude.

While your main function is to find and screen good candidates, your other aim is to attract them to your firm. A sincere and informal attitude, respect for the applicant as an individual, and prompt follow – up letters can help you to sell the employer to the interviewee.

1. College recruiting is an important source of the following people except _____ .

A. management trainees

B. management trainers

C. professional employees

D. technical employees

2. Which of the following isn't the weakness of college recruiting? _____ .

A. It is relatively expensive

B. It is relatively time – consuming

C. It is sometimes ineffective

D. Its main function is screening

3. According to the passage, goals of a campus recruiter include the following except _____ .

A. screening

B. determining whether a candidate is worthy of further consideration

C. printing company brochures

D. attracting candidates to your firm

4. According to the passage, the author might most likely agree that _____ .

A. college recruiting can find and screen many good candidates

B. there is no problem with college recruiting

C. it is unnecessary to train recruiters before college recruiting

D. it isn't the goal of a campus recruiter to sell the employer to the interviewee

5. This passage mainly discussed _____ .

A. the problems and goals of college recruiting

B. the problems of college recruiting

C. the goals of college recruiting

D. the methods of college recruiting

(二)

The managerial grid training as developed by Blake and his colleagues consists of a simple diagnostic framework provided to members to aid them in describing one another's behavior.

The basis philosophy of grid training is that the task of the individual manager is to achieve production through people. In achieving this task, the manager has to show concern both for productivity and people.

Blake suggests that managers can be characterized by their location on a two – dimensional grid, the managerial grid—one axis of which is labeled concern for production and the other concern for people. Each axis is a scale with nine points and so the location of a manager on the grid can be specified by two coordinates. The five principal managerial styles as described in Blake's grid are:

(1) Improved management—exertion et minimum offer to get done the work required to maintain membership of the organization.

(2) Task management where a person is high in task efficiency but low in human satisfaction.

(3) Team management—high task achievement from committed people. Production is achieved by the integration of task and human requirements into a unified system.

A grid seminar is used to teach each participant to see his or her managerial style. Trainees are first familiarized with grid language and theory and then work in groups through a series of exercises and case problems that allow each individual to exhibit management style. This behavior then becomes the object of feedback. Trainees acquire skills in the perception of their own and other people's styles of behavior, and the aim is to move them toward the 9, 9 region of the grid.

Grid training consists of a series of seminars intended to develop the application of the message throughout the organization. In this respect, it is a type of organization development "intervention" designed to increase organizational effectiveness rather than to concentrate on the improvement of individual interactive skills.

The grid has sound theoretical foundations, being based on a number of research studies. It recognizes the importance of developing an appropriate management style to obtain results by the effort an commitment of work groups. It has plenty of fact validity—ex – grid trainees usually speak highly of it—but research studies are only partially conclusive on its overall effectiveness.

1. The basis philosophy of the managerial grid training is that _____ .

A. the task of the individual manager is to achieve people through production

B. the task of the individual manager is to achieve production through people

C. the task of the individuals is to achieve production through other people

D. the task of the individual manager is to achieve production through himself (herself)

2. Whih of the following statements on the managerial grid is false? _____ .

A. It is a two – dimensional grid

B. One axis of it is labeled concern for production and the other concern for people

C. Each axis is a scale with nine points

D. The location of a manager on the grid can be specified by two or more coordinates

3. From the passage, we can draw conclusions on managerial styles as described in Blake's grid except _____ .

A. 1, 1 indicates where a person is low in both task efficiency and human satisfaction

B. 1, 9 indicates where a person is high in task efficiency but low in human satisfaction

C. 5, 5 where a person is middle in both task efficiency and human satisfaction

D. 9, 1 indicates where a person is high in task efficiency but low in human satisfaction

4. About a grid seminar, the author would disagree that _____ .

A. a grid seminar is used to teach each participant to see his or her managerial style

B. trainees are first familiarized with grid language and theory

C. trainees can't perceive their own style of behavior

D. the aim is to move trainees toward the 9, 9 region of the grid

5. This passage may be extracted from the paper which studied _____ .

A. training

B. performance appraisal

C. compensation

D. HR planning

第八篇 专业英语模拟试卷 8

一、英汉互译（每题 2 分，共 30 分）

1. Apprenticeship

2. Competitive advantage

3. Employee empowerment

4. Formal education programs

5. Internal growth strategy

6. Job progressions

7. Management by objectives（MBO）

8. Performance feedback

9. Replacement charts

10. Strategic congruence

11. 网上培训

12. 招募

13. 工资结构

14. 劳动力市场

15. 奖金

二、选词填空（每题 2 分，共 20 分）

A. profit – sharing	B. goals	C. job satisfaction
D. off – the – job	E. skills analysis	F. benefit program
G. interviews	H. outcomes	I. feedback J. mediation

1. Job instruction techniques should be based on _____ and learning theory.

2. Desire can be created by amplifying the job's interest factors plus extras such as _____, career development, travel, or similar advantages.

3. Tests, application blanks, and _____ should be a proven part of the employer's selection process.

4. With _____ a neutral third party tries to assist the principals in reaching agreement.

5. Organizational rewards should be linked to each individual employee's _____.

6. The flexible benefits can turn the traditional homogeneous _____ into a motivator.

7. Piece – rate, wage incentive plans, _____, and lump – sum bonuses are all forms of performance – based compensation.

8. Evaluation is the comparison of objectives with _____ to answer the question of how far the training has achieved its purpose.

9. Case study is an _____ training technique.

10. Coaching should provide motivation, structure, and effective _____, if the coacher is skilled, dedicated, and able to develop mutual confidence.

三、单项选择题（每题 2 分，共 20 分）

1. The placement of an employee in another job for which the duties, responsibilities, status, and remuneration are approximately equal to those of the previous job is known as a _____ .

A. promotion

B. transfer

C. lateral move

D. job rotation

2. If employees' pay is based not on the actual amount of time it takes them to complete a job but on a predetermined amount of time for completing the job, which incentive plan are they working under? _____ .

A. Piece – rate plan

B. Standard hour plan

C. Time division plan

D. Completion pay system

3. Of the following, the one that would not be considered a chief objective of most benefits programs is _____ .

A. reducing turnover

B. improving employee satisfaction

C. "sidestepping" legal requirements for employee health and safety

D. attracting and motivating employees

4. The term used to refer to the language, religion, values and attitudes, politics, technology, education, and social organization of a nation is _____ .

A. ritual environment

B. general environment

C. cultural environment

D. task environment

5. Which of the following is not a typical method of increasing the power of employees? _____ .

A. Job enlargement

B. Enrichment

C. Standardization

D. Relying on self – managed teams

6. Which management group has primary responsibility for the development of disciplinary policies and procedures? _____ .

A. The legal department

B. Top – level management

C. The HR department

D. Middle management

7. Which of the following is not a phase of a system model of training? _____ .

A. Needs assessment

B. Motivation assessment

C. Program implementation

D. Evaluation

8. Which of the following is not a primary impact that technology has had on HRM? _____ .

A. It has altered the methods of collecting employment information

B. It has sped up the processing of employment data

C. It has diminished the role of supervisors in managing employees

D. It has improved the processes of internal and external communications

9. A pictorial representation of all organizational jobs along with the numbers of employees currently occupying those jobs and future employment requirements is called _____ .

A. a staffing table

B. an organization chart

C. a skills inventory

D. career planning

10. When determining where training emphasis should be placed, an examination of the goals, resources, and environment of the organization is known as _____ .

A. task analysis

B. organization analysis

C. resource analysis

D. skills analysis

四、阅读理解（每题 3 分，共 30 分）

（一）

In collective bargaining, an impasse occurs when the parties are not able to move further toward settlement. An impasse usually occurs because one party is demanding more than the other will offer. Sometimes an impasse can be resolved through a third party, a disinterested person such as a mediator or arbitrator. If the impasse is not resolved in this way, a work stoppage, or strike, may be called by the union to bring pressure to bear on management.

Three types of third – party interventions are used to overcome an impasse: Mediation, fact – finding, and arbitration. With mediation a neutral third party tries to assist the principals in reaching agreement. The mediator usually holds meetings with each party to determine where each stands regarding its position, and then this information is used to find common ground for further bargaining. The mediator is always a go – between. As such, he or she communicates assessments of the likelihood of a strike, the possible settlement packages available, and the like. The mediator does not have the authority to fix a position or make a concession.

In certain situations as in a national emergency dispute where the president of the United States determines that it would be a national emergency for a strike to occur, a fact – finder may be appointed. A fact – finder is a neutral party who studies the issues in a dispute and makes a public recommendation of what a reasonable settlement ought to be. For example, presidential emergency fact – finding boards have successfully resolved impasses in certain critical transportation disputes.

Arbitration is the most definitive type of third – party intervention, since the arbitrator often has the power to determine and dictate the settlement terms. Unlike mediation and fact – finding, arbitration can guarantee a solution to an impasse. With binding arbitration, both parties are committed to accepting the arbitrator's award. With non – binding arbitration, they are not. Arbitration may also be voluntary or compulsory (in other words, imposed by a government agency) . In the United States, voluntary binding arbitration is the most prevalent.

1. Which of the following statements about an impasse in collective bargaining is

false? _____ .

A. An impasse occurs when the parties are not able to reach an agreement

B. An impasse usually occurs when one party is demanding more than the other will offer

C. An impasse can be resolved through a mediator or arbitrator

D. If the impasse is not resolved, the union can't bring pressure to bear on management

2. The types of third – party interventions which can be used to overcome an impasse include the following except _____ .

A. arbitration

B. fact – finding

C. strike

D. mediation

3. From this passage, we can't draw a conclusion on the mediator that _____ .

A. the mediator tries to assist the principals in reaching agreement

B. the mediator usually holds meetings with each party to determine where each stands regarding its position

C. the mediator is always a go – between

D. the mediator has the authority to fix a position or make a concession

4. According to the passage, we can infer that _____ .

A. the president of the United States has the right to determine that a national emergency dispute would be a national emergency for a strike to occur

B. the arbitrator has no right to determine and dictate the settlement terms

C. mediation and fact – finding can also ensure a solution to an impasse

D. in the United States, compulsory binding arbitration is the most popular

5. The best title for the passage might be _____ .

A. third – party interventions

B. impasse

C. impasse and third – party interventions

D. arbitration and mediation

(二)

Many employers today are supplementing their permanent employee base by hiring contingent workers. Also defined as temporary workers, part – time workers, and just – in – time employees, the contingent work force is big and growing and is broadly defined as workers who don't have permanent jobs.

Just how big is the contingent work force? One way to answer that is to note that in 1993, part – time workers (those employed for less than 35 hours per week) numbered 21 million, or about 17% of the U. S. labor force. Slicing the numbers another way, in 1993 there were 1. 7 million people working in the temporary help industry (for temporary help firms like Manpower, Inc. and Kelly Services) , up from 732000 in 1985. Temporary jobs represented 20% of all the new jobs created in the United States between 1991 and 1993.

Contingent staffing owes its growing popularity to several factors. Historically, employers have always used "temps" to fill in for the days or weeks that permanent employees were out sick or on vacation. Increasingly, however, a desire for ever – higher productivity probably explains its growing popularity. In general, as one expert puts it, "productivity is measured in terms of output per hour paid for" ... and "if employees are paid only when they're working, as contingent workers are, overall productivity increases" . Employers also find that by tapping temporary help agencies, they can save the time and expense of personally recruiting and training new workers, as well as the expenses involved in personnel documentation (such as filing payroll taxes and maintaining absence records). As a result, the contingent work force is no longer limited to clerical or maintenance staff: in one recent year almost 100000 people found temporary work in engineering, science, or management support occupations, for instance. In fact, growing numbers of firms use temporary workers such as engineers and other professionals to carry out engineering projects, to staff hospitals to meet fluctuating patient loads, and to serve as short – term chief financial officers, for instance.

1. Which of the following isn't contingent workers? _____ .

A. Temporary workers

B. Part – time workers

C. Permanent employees

D. Just – in – time employees

2. About the number or percentage of contingent workers in the U. S. in 1993, which of the following is false? _____ .

A. 21 million

B. 17% of the U. S. labor force

C. Slicing the numbers another way, there were 1. 7 million

D. 20% of employees who worked for all the new jobs

3. Contingent workers are now growing popular because of the following factors except _____ .

A. employers desire for ever – higher productivity

B. employers want to fill in for the days or weeks that permanent employees are on vacation

C. employers can save the time and expense of personally recruiting and training new workers

D. employers can save the expenses involved in filing payroll taxes and maintaining absence records

4. According to the passage, there are several job areas for contingent workers except _____ .

A. permanent jobs

B. maintenance

C. engineering

D. management support occupations

5. This passage might be extracted from the paper about _____ .

A. selection

B. recruitment

C. outplacement

D. replacement

第九篇　专业英语模拟试卷 9

一、英汉互译（每题 2 分，共 30 分）

1. Boycott

2. Cultural environment

3. Factor comparison system

4. Job posting and bidding

5. Leaderless group discussion

6. Outsourcing

7. Point system

8. Situational interview

9. Strategic human resource management（SHRM）

10. Skill – based pay

11. 任务分析

12. 绩效管理

13. 工作满意度

14. 全球化

15. 仲裁

二、选词填空（每题 2 分，共 20 分）

A. skills	B. job description	C. interaction
D. management	E. role playing	F. work force
G. discipline	H. rewards	I. task J. training

1. Developing a high – trust organization means creating trust between _____ and employees.

2. Retaining knowledge workers is a matter of providing a supportive workplace environment and motivating them through both tangible and intangible _____ .

3. Increased _____ diversity will place tremendous demands on the HR management function.

4. Writing _____ and job specification based on input from department supervisor is the responsibility of HR department.

5. Supervisors should make sure employees are guaranteed fair treatment as it relates to _____ , dismissal and job security.

6. It is important to evaluate _____ in order to assess its effectiveness in producing the learning outcomes.

7. Job rotation can be an inefficient and frustrating method of acquiring additional knowledge and _____ unless it is carefully planned and controlled.

8. In _____ the participants act out a situation by assuming the roles of the characters involved.

9. The basis philosophy of managerial grid training is that the _____ of the individual manager is to achieve production through people.

10. Interactive skills training is defined by Rackham as: "Any form of training which aims to increase the effectiveness of an individual's _____ with others."

三、单项选择题（每题 2 分，共 20 分）

1. An example of a qualitative approach to demand forecasting is _____ .

A. trend analysis

B. the Delphi technique

C. multiple predictive models

D. modeling

2. Services that are offered to employees who are being transferred to different locations are known as _____ .

A. outplacement services

B. relocation services

C. transfer services

D. adjustment services

3. Self – appraisals are best for _____ .

A. administrative purposes

B. developmental purposes

C. promotional purposes

D. regulatory purposes

4. The point system permits jobs to be evaluated on the basis of elements known as _____ .

A. description factors

B. compensable factors

C. skill factors

D. knowledge factors

5. Sometimes organizations provide services to terminated employees that help them bridge the gap between their old position and a new job. These services are known as _____ .

A. downsizing programs

B. "headhunting" assistance programs

C. outplacement assistance

D. employee assistance programs（EAPs）

6. Consultation provided by HR staff should not _____ .

A. be based on managerial expertise

B. be based on technical expertise

C. help managers or supervisors make firm decisions

D. conflict with the goals of the managers or supervisors seeking assistance

7. The examination of the attitudes and activities of a company's workforce refers to _____ .

A. environmental scanning

B. performing a trend analysis

C. performing a cultural audit

D. behavioral modeling

8. When a combination salary and commission plan is used to compensate sales employees, the percentage of cash compensation paid in commission is called _____ .

A. a bonus

B. a lump – sum bonus

C. an incentive

D. leverage

9. The two principal criteria for determining promotions are _____ .

A. seniority and salary

B. knowledge and skills

C. seniority and knowledge

D. merit and seniority

10. When the multinational corporation sends employees from its home country, these employees are referred to as _____ .

A. host – country nationals

B. third – country nationals

C. international managers

D. expatriates

四、阅读理解（每题 3 分，共 30 分）

（一）

Japanese management gives a great deal of attention to orientation and training, which is particularly true in the case of regular employees. Pre – employment education generally starts immediately after the person is chosen. The purpose of the program is to (a) familiarize the student with the company; (b) monitor the person's activities; (c) make the student comfortable with the company; (d) answer questions the person might have; and (e) provide the new hirers with any basic skills training the company feels they require.

The appraisal and compensation system is long – term in orientation and is based on rewarding people for doing a good job over an extended period of time. In the United States employees commonly receive an annual appraisal that indicates whether or not they are doing a good job and, if not, provides feedback related to improving performance or seeking employment elsewhere. In Japan the initial apprais-al is typically given at the end of a 7 – 10 year period. At this point the person learns whether or not he or she is going to be promoted up the ranks of management or not. Those who fail this first major evaluation know that their chances of making the top management ranks are virtually nil.

Compensation in Japan used to be based heavily on seniority, but today merit is becoming more important. In many industries the annual raise is in the 2 – 4 percent range and often is based heavily on merit factors such as attitude, ability, and coop-erativeness. Another feature that distinguishes the Japanese system form many others is the semiannual bonus or wage allowance. This bonus is separate from the annual wage increase and, usually without exception, is paid every year regardless of the state of the economy. The bonus is typically equivalent to 5 – 6 months' salary and is paid in midsummer and at the end of the year. Other forms of compensation include housing allowances, daily living support for transportation, meals, uniforms, health care, and cultural and recreational benefits.

1. The purposes of pre – employment education in Japan don't include _____ .

A. familiarizing the student with the company

B. monitor the person's activities

C. make the student comfortable with the company

D. provide the new hirers with any knowledge and skills

2. The appraisal and compensation system in Japan is based on _____ .

A. rewarding people for doing a good job over an extended period of time

B. rewarding people for doing a good job over a year

C. rewarding people for doing any job over a long time

D. rewarding people for doing any job over a year

3. In Japan the initial appraisal is typically given at the end of a _____ year period.

A. 5 – 10

B. 7 – 10

C. 10 – 12

D. 10 – 15

4. About compensation in Japan, the author would disagree that _____ .

A. compensation in Japan are based heavily on merit today

B. merit factors include attitude, ability, and cooperativeness

C. the main feature that distinguishes the Japanese system form many others is the semiannual bonus or wage allowance

D. the semiannual bonus equals to 5 – 6 months' salary

5. From this passage, we can't conclude that _____ .

A. in Japan, working for a long time in a company is beneficial to employees

B. the orientation of appraisal and compensation system in Japan is different from the one in the United States

C. in the United States, employees who commonly receive an annual appraisal can't know whether or not they are doing a good job

D. employees in Japan may get housing allowances, daily living support for transportation, meals, uniforms, health care, and cultural and recreational benefits

(二)

Recruiting is important, because the more applicants you have the more selective you can be in your hiring. If only two candidates apply for two openings, you may have little choice but to hire them. But if 10 or 20 applicants appear, then you can employ techniques like interviews and tests to screen out all but the best.

Some employers use a recruiting yield pyramid to calculate the number of applicants they must generate to hire the required number of new employees. In figure 1, the company knows 50 new entry – level accountants must be hired next year. From experience, the firm also knows that the ratio of offers made to actual new hires is 2 to 1; about half the people to whom offers are made accept. Similarly, the firm knows that the ratio of candidates interviewed to offers made is 3 to 2, while the ratio of candidates invited for interviews to candidates actually interviewed has been 4 to 3. Finally, the firm knows that the ratio of new leads generated to candidates actually invited has been 6 to 1; in other words, of six leads that come in from the firm's advertising college recruiting, and other recruiting efforts, one applicant in six typically is invited to come for an interview. Given these ratios, the firm knows it must generate 1200 leads to be able to invite 200 viable candidates to its offices for interviews. The firm will then get to interview about 150 of those invited, and from these it will make 100 offers. Of those 100 offers, half (or 50 new CPAs) will be hired.

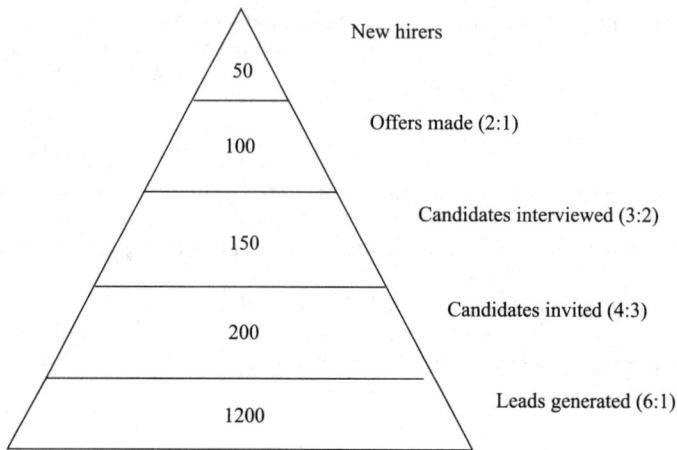

Recruiting Yield Pyramid

The quality of a firm's recruiting process had a big impact on what candidates thought of the firm. For example, when asked after the initial job interview why they thought a particular company might be a good fit, all 41 mentioned the nature of the job; however, 12 also mentioned the impression made by the recruiters themselves and 9 said the comments of friends and acquaintances affected their impressions. Unfortunately, the reverse was also true. When asked why they judged some firms as bad fits, 39 mentioned the nature of the job, but 23 said they'd been turned off by recruiters. For example, some were dressed sloppily; others were "barely literate"; some were rude; and some made offensively sexist comments.

1. A recruiting yield pyramid might include the following except _____ .

A. offers made

B. candidates rewarded

C. candidates interviewed

D. leads generated

2. According to the recruiting yield pyramid, if the ratio of new leads generated to candidates actually invited is 5 to 1, the ratio of candidates invited for interviews to candidates actually interviewed is 2 to 1, and the firm want to interview about 100 of those invited, then the firm must generate _____ leads.

A. 200

B. 500

C. 1000

D. 1200

3. According to the recruiting yield pyramid, if the ratio of offers made to actual new hires is 3 to 2, the ratio of candidates interviewed to offers made is 5 to 3, and the firm had interviewed 500, then it can hire _____ .

A. 50

B. 100

C. 150

D. 200

4. From the passage, we can infer that _____ .

A. if only two candidates apply for two openings, you can employ techniques like interviews and tests

B. the quality of a firm's recruiting process can influence what candidates thought of the firm

C. the more applicants you have, the worse your recruitment might become

D. a recruiting yield pyramid can't be used to calculate the number of applicants they must generate to hire the required number of new employees

5. The best title for this passage might be _____ .

A. introduction of recruiting

B. recruiting yield pyramid

C. the quality of recruiting process

D. significance of recruiting

第十篇　专业英语模拟试卷 10

一、英汉互译（每题 2 分，共 30 分）

1. Benchmarks

2. Downward move

3. Gain sharing plans

4. Internal analysis

5. Job ranking system

6. Merit guideline

7. Peer appraisal

8. Reengineering

9. Role ambiguity

10. Team leader training

11. 自我评估

12. 晋升

13. 学习型组织

14. 反馈

15. 奖金

二、选词填空（每题2分，共20分）

A. workforce	B. absenteeism	C. orientation
D. benefit	E. questionnaire	F. downsizing
G. perquisites	H. input	I. performance　J. satisfaction

1. The appraisal and compensation system is long – term in _____ and is based on rewarding people for doing a good job over an extended period of time.

2. The organization will provide employees with indirect compensations insurance, pay for holidays and vacations, services, and _____.

3. Individuals should perceive a strong relationship between their _____ and the rewards they receive if motivation is to be maximized.

4. Flexible benefits allow employees to pick and choose from among a menu of _____ options.

5. Satisfied and committed employees have lower rates of turnover and _____.

6. Business process re – engineering techniques are deployed as instruments for _____.

7. A forecast is needed of the amount by which the _____ has to be reduced and the likely losses through employee turnover.

8. 360 – degree feedback recognizes the complexity of management and the value of _____ from various sources.

9. 360 – degree feedback is most likely to be successful when items covered in

the _____ can be related to actual events experienced by the individual.

10. When pay is seen as fair based on job demands, individual skill level, and community pay standards, _____ is likely to result.

三、单项选择题 （每题 2 分，共 20 分）

1. Executives or managers who coach, advise, and encourage employees of lesser rank are called _____ .

A. protégés

B. teachers

C. mentors

D. role models

2. Objectives accomplished through job analysis include all of the following except _____ .

A. establishing the job – relatedness of selection requirements

B. determining the relative worth of a job

C. eliminating discrepancies between internal wage rates and market rates

D. proving criteria for evaluating the performance of an employee

3. Staffing the organization, designing jobs and teams, developing skillful employees, identifying approaches for improving employee performance, and other "HRM" issues are duties typically reserved for _____ .

A. HR managers

B. line managers

C. HR and line managers

D. top executives

4. 360 – degree feedback might be used for the following except _____ .

A. personal development

B. appraisal

C. pay

D. recruitment

5. An employer wishing to set up the job classification system of job evaluation would have to _____ .

A. establish a point plan to evaluate all jobs

B. rank jobs according to the beliefs of committee members

C. describe job grades with increasing amount of responsibility, skill, knowledge, or ability

D. evaluate jobs with the use of a job evaluation scale

6. Which of the following isn't a form of performance – based compensation? _____ .

A. Piece – rate

B. Profit – sharing

C. Minimum wage

D. Lump – sum bonuses

7. The performance measures that might be used for performance – based compensation include the following except _____ .

A. individual work time

B. departmental productivity

C. unit profitability

D. the overall organization's profitability

8. Coaching is a _____ technique that can be used to develop individual skills,

knowledge, and attitudes.

A. on – the – job

B. off – the – job

C. web – based training

D. classroom training

9. An organization wishing to establish greater job – staffing flexibility would likely use which pay system? _____ .

A. Straight pay

B. Skill – based pay

C. Incentive pay

D. Two – tier pay

10. Human capital of a firm include the following except _____ .

A. the knowledge of a firm's workers

B. skills of a firm's workers

C. the expertise of a firm's workers

D. the behavior of a firm's workers

四、阅读理解（每题 3 分，共 30 分）

（一）

Bargaining in good faith is the cornerstone of effective labor management relations. It means that both parties communicate and negotiate. It means that proposals are matched with counterproposals and that both parties make every reasonable effort to arrive at an agreement. It does not mean that either party is compelled to agree to a proposal. Nor does it require that either party make any specific concessions.

When is bargaining not in good faith? As interpreted by the NLRB and the courts, a violation of the requirement for good faith bargaining may include the following:

(1) *Surface bargaining.* This involves merely going through the motions of bargaining without any real intention of completing a formal agreement.

(2) *Concession.* Although no one is required to make a concession, the court's and NLRB's definitions of good faith suggest that a willingness to compromise is an essential ingredient in good faith bargaining.

(3) *Proposals and demands.* The NLRB considers the advancement of proposals as a positive factor in determining overall good faith.

(4) *Dilatory tactics.* The law requires that the parties meet and "confer at reasonable times and intervals". Obviously, refusal to meet at all with the union does not satisfy the positive duty imposed on the employer.

(5) *Imposing conditions.* Attempts to impose conditions that are so onerous or unreasonable as to indicate bad faith will be scrutinized by the board.

(6) *Unilateral changes in conditions.* This is viewed as a strong indication that the employer is not bargaining with the required intent of reaching an agreement.

(7) *Bypassing the representative.* An employer violates its duty to bargain when it refuses to negotiate with the union representative. The duty of management to bargain in good faith involves, at a minimum, recognition that this statutory representative is the one with whom the employer must deal in conducting bargaining negotiations.

(8) *Commission of unfair labor practices during negotiations.* Such practices may reflect poorly upon the good faith of the guilty party.

（9）*Providing information.* Information must be supplied to the union, upon request, to enable it to understand and intelligently discuss the issues raised in bargaining.

（10）*Bargaining items.* Refusal to bargain on a mandatory item（one must bargain over these）or insistence on a permissive item（one may bargain over these）is usually viewed as bad faith bargaining.

1. Bargaining in good faith does not mean that _____ .

A. both parties communicate and negotiate

B. proposals are in line with counterproposals

C. both parties make great effort to reach an agreement

D. either party must agree to a proposal

2. According to the interpretion of the NLRB and the courts, bargaining may be in good faith when _____ .

A. both parties have no real intention of completing a formal agreement

B. both parties are willing to compromise

C. employers refuse to meet with the union

D. both parties attempt to impose unreasonable conditions

3. Which of the following isn't a positive factor in determining overall good faith? _____ .

A. A willingness to compromise

B. The advancement of proposals

C. Unilateral changes in conditions

D. Providing information

4. From this passage, we can conclude that _____ .

A. it isn't mandatory to meet and "confer at reasonable times and intervals" for both parties

B. employers can refuse to negotiate with the union representative in order to bargain in good faith

C. commission of unfair labor practices during negotiations may reflect little good faith of the guilty party

D. insistence on a permissive item can bring bargaining in good faith

5. The best title for the passage might be _____ .

A. what is and when is not bargaining in good faith

B. what is bargaining in good faith

C. when is not bargaining in good faith

D. how to bargain in good faith

（二）

Fewer 18 - to 25 - year - olds are entering the work force; this has caused many employers to look into "harnessing America's gray power". Is it practical in terms of productivity to keep older workers on? The answer seems unequivocably to be "yes". Age - related changes in physical ability, cognitive performance, and personality have little effect on worker's output except in the most physically deman-ding tasks. Similarly , creative and intellectual achievements do not decline with age and absenteeism drops as age increases. Older workers also usually display more company loyalty than youthful workers, tend to be more satisfied with their jobs and supervision, and can be trained or retrained as effectively as anyone.

Recruiting and attracting older workers generally requires a comprehensive HR retiree effort before the recruiting begins. The aim is to make the company an attrac-tive place in which the older worker can work. Specifically:

Examine your personnel policies. Check to make sure policies and procedures do not discourage recruitment of seniors or encourage valuable older people to leave.

Develop flexible work options. These include part – time, shorter – than – 30 – hour workweeks, consulting or seasonal work, reduced hours with reduced pay, and flextime.

Create or redesign suitable jobs. At Xerox, unionized hourly workers over 55 with 15 years of service and those over 50 with 20 years of service can bid on jobs at lower stress and lower pay levels if they so desire.

Offer or redesign suitable jobs. Allowing employees to pick and choose among benefit options can be attractive to older as well as younger employees.

As one expert puts it, to recruit older workers, the message must be tailored to their way of thinking. Appealing to job qualities they value will attract attention. These include flexible hours, flexible benefits, autonomy, opportunity to meet new friends, and working with people their own age. You might also stress that you value their maturity and experience.

1. Which of the age – related changes will affect worker's output except in the most physically demanding tasks? _____ .

A. Physical ability

B. Cognitive performance

C. Personality

D. Company loyalty

2. "Harnessing America's gray power", means that _____ .

A. keeping older workers on

B. recruiting 18 – to 25 – year – olds

C. attracting minorities

D. encouraging women to enter the work force

3. In order to make the company an attractive place in which the older worker can work, HR staff should do the following except _____ .

A. examine the personnel policies

B. develop flexible work options

C. reward at lower pay levels

D. offer or redesign suitable jobs

4. According to the passage, which of the following isn't a flexible work option? _____ .

A. Shorter – than – 30 – hour workweeks

B. Full – time

C. Seasonal work

D. Reduced hours with reduced pay

5. From this passage, we can infer that _____ .

A. in America, there is no deficit of work force

B. absenteeism is positively related to ages

C. flexible work options can be attractive to older workers

D. to recruit older workers, the message needn't be in accordance with their way of thinking

附录1 《企业人力资源管理师》(三级) 理论知识鉴定要素细目表

职业（工种）					企业人力资源管理师		等级	三级	
职业代码									
序号	鉴定点代码				鉴定内容	分数系数	重要系数	备注	
	章	节	目	点					
	1				**人力资源规划**	18			
	1	**1**			**人力资源预测**		5		
	1	1	1		人力资源信息分析		5		
1	1	1	1	1	人力资源信息		5		
2	1	1	1	2	人力资源信息的分析过程		5		
3	1	1	1	3	人力资源信息的审核		1		
4	1	1	1	4	人力资源信息分析方法		5		
5	1	1	1	5	人力资源信息分析报告的撰写		5		
	1	1	2		人力资源需求预测		5		
6	1	1	2	1	人力资源需求的影响因素		5		
7	1	1	2	2	人力资源需求预测方法		5		
8	1	1	2	3	人力资源需求预测步骤		5		
	1	1	3		人力资源供给预测		5		
9	1	1	3	1	人力资源供给的影响因素		5		
10	1	1	3	2	人力资源供给预测方法		5		
11	1	1	3	3	人力资源供给预测步骤		5		

297

续表

序号	鉴定点代码				鉴定内容	分数系数	重要系数	备注
	章	节	目	点				
	1	1	4		人力资源供求平衡		5	
12	1	1	4	1	人力资源供求平衡的影响因素		5	
13	1	1	4	2	人力资源供求动态平衡		5	
	1	**2**			**人力资源管理制度建设**		5	
	1	2	1		人力资源管理制度概述		1	
14	1	2	1	1	人力资源管理制度的构成		1	
15	1	2	1	2	人力资源管理制度的特征		5	
16	1	2	1	3	人力资源管理制度的基本要求		5	
	1	2	2		人力资源管理制度建设		5	
17	1	2	2	1	人力资源管理制度建设的原则		1	
18	1	2	2	2	人力资源管理制度建设的程序		5	
19	1	2	2	3	人力资源管理制度建设的步骤		5	
	1	**3**			**工作设计与工作分析**		9	
	1	3	1		工作设计		5	
20	1	3	1	1	工作设计的概念		1	
21	1	3	1	2	工作设计的原则		5	
22	1	3	1	3	工作设计的内容		5	
23	1	3	1	4	工作设计的方法		5	
24	1	3	1	5	岗位设置的形式		1	
	1	3	2		工作分析		9	
25	1	3	2	1	工作分析的主体		5	
26	1	3	2	2	工作分析的流程		5	
	1	3	3		工作说明书编制		9	
27	1	3	3	1	工作描述		5	
28	1	3	3	2	工作规范		5	
29	1	3	3	3	工作说明书的编制要求		9	
30	1	3	3	4	工作说明书的内容安排		9	

职业（工种）：企业人力资源管理师　等级：三级
职业代码：

职业（工种）				企业人力资源管理师	等级		三级	
职业代码								
序号	鉴定点代码				鉴定内容	分数系数	重要系数	备注
	章	节	目	点				
	2				**招聘与配置**	20		
	2	**1**			**招聘计划与实施**		5	
	2	1	1		招聘计划		9	
31	2	1	1	1	招聘计划的制订		9	
32	2	1	1	2	招聘计划的内容与修订		5	
33	2	1	1	3	招聘计划的审批与实施控制		5	
	2	1	2		招聘来源和渠道		5	
34	2	1	2	1	内部招聘的概念和方法		5	
35	2	1	2	2	外部招聘的概念和方法		5	
	2	1	3		招聘广告		5	
36	2	1	3	1	招聘广告设计的基本原则		5	
37	2	1	3	2	招聘广告的内容		5	
	2	**2**			**招聘选拔**		9	
	2	2	1		知识测验		5	
38	2	2	1	1	知识测验概述		1	
39	2	2	1	2	知识测验的优缺点		5	
40	2	2	1	3	知识测验题的编制		1	
41	2	2	1	4	知识测验的实施		5	
	2	2	2		心理测验		5	
42	2	2	2	1	心理测验的特点		5	
43	2	2	2	2	心理测验对员工招聘的意义		5	
44	2	2	2	3	招聘中的心理测验应用类型		1	
45	2	2	2	4	招聘测评中的心理测验实施步骤		5	
	2	2	3		招聘面试		9	
46	2	2	3	1	结构化面试		9	
47	2	2	3	2	面试流程的管理		9	
	2	**3**			**人员录用**		9	
	2	3	1		人员录用概述		5	
48	2	3	1	1	人员录用的原则		1	
49	2	3	1	2	人员录用的要求		5	
50	2	3	1	3	人员录用基本步骤		5	

续表

职业（工种）				企业人力资源管理师		等级		三级
职业代码								

序号	鉴定点代码				鉴定内容	分数系数	重要系数	备注
	章	节	目	点				
	2	3	2		人员录用决策		5	
51	2	3	2	1	人员录用的决策		5	
52	2	3	2	2	录用决策的方法		9	
	2	3	3		人员录用实施		9	
53	2	3	3	1	人员录用通知		9	
54	2	3	3	2	办理入职手续		9	
55	2	3	3	3	签订劳动合同		1	
56	2	3	3	4	进行新员工培训		1	
57	2	3	3	5	试用期管理		5	
	2	**4**			**人员配置与离职管理**		5	
	2	4	1		人员配置		5	
58	2	4	1	1	人员配置的原则		1	
59	2	4	1	2	人员配置的匹配原理		5	
60	2	4	1	3	人员配置的类型		**5**	
	2	4	2		离职管理		5	
61	2	4	2	1	离职管理的原则		1	
62	2	4	2	2	离职原因分析		5	
63	2	4	2	3	离职面谈		5	
	3				**培训与开发**	20		
	3	**1**			**培训需求分析**		5	
	3	1	1		培训需求分析概述		5	
64	3	1	1	1	培训需求分析的概念		1	
65	3	1	1	2	培训需求分析的作用		1	
66	3	1	1	3	培训需求分析的层面		5	
67	3	1	1	4	培训需求分析的时机		5	
68	3	1	1	5	培训需求分析中的常见误区		1	
	3	1	2		培训需求分析实施		5	

续表

职业（工种）				企业人力资源管理师	等级		三级	
职业代码								
序号	鉴定点代码				鉴定内容	分数系数	重要系数	备注
	章	节	目	点				
69	3	1	2	1	培训需求分析的准备		5	
70	3	1	2	2	培训需求的调查		5	
71	3	1	2	3	调查需求的确认		5	
72	3	1	2	4	培训需求分析报告的撰写		5	
	3	**2**			**培训计划制订**		5	
	3	2	1		培训目标设计		5	
73	3	2	1	1	培训目标及其构成要素		5	
74	3	2	1	2	确定培训目标的意义		1	
75	3	2	1	3	培训目标的确定		1	
	3	2	2		培训计划的编制		5	
76	3	2	2	1	培训计划		5	
77	3	2	2	2	培训计划的分类		1	
78	3	2	2	3	培训计划的内容		5	
79	3	2	2	4	培训计划的制订程序		5	
	3	**3**			**培训的组织实施**		9	
	3	3	1		培训方法的选择与运用		5	
80	3	3	1	1	培训方法的比较		1	
81	3	3	1	2	培训方法的选择		5	
	3	3	2		培训师的选择与培训		5	
82	3	3	2	1	培训师的要求		5	
83	3	3	2	2	培训师的类型		1	
84	3	3	2	3	培训师的选择		5	
85	3	3	2	4	培训师的培训		5	
	3	3	3		培训机构的选择		5	
86	3	3	3	1	培训机构的选择步骤		5	
87	3	3	3	2	考察培训机构需要注意的问题		1	
	3	3	4		培训预算编制		5	

职业（工种）				企业人力资源管理师	等级		三级	
职业代码								
序号	鉴定点代码				鉴定内容	分数系数	重要系数	备注
	章	节	目	点				
88	3	3	4	1	培训预算的构成		5	
89	3	3	4	2	培训预算的原则		5	
90	3	3	4	3	培训预算的流程		5	
91	3	3	4	4	培训预算的确定方法		5	
92	3	3	4	5	培训预算的工作要点		1	
	4				**绩效管理**	18		
	4	**1**			**绩效计划**		9	
	4	1	1		绩效计划制订		5	
93	4	1	1	1	绩效计划及其作用		1	
94	4	1	1	2	绩效计划的主要内容		5	
95	4	1	1	3	绩效计划的相关主体		5	
96	4	1	1	4	绩效计划的制订原则		1	
97	4	1	1	5	绩效计划的制订流程		5	
	4	1	2		绩效目标设定		5	
98	4	1	2	1	绩效目标		1	
99	4	1	2	2	绩效目标分解		5	
100	4	1	2	3	绩效目标确定		5	
	4	1	3		绩效指标设计		9	
101	4	1	3	1	绩效及其影响因素		5	
102	4	1	3	2	绩效指标的要素		1	
103	4	1	3	3	绩效指标的类型		1	
104	4	1	3	4	绩效指标设计的原则		1	
105	4	1	3	5	绩效指标设计的流程		9	
	4	**2**			**绩效评估实施**		5	
	4	2	1		绩效评估方法		5	
106	4	2	1	1	目标管理法		5	
107	4	2	1	2	行为锚定法		5	

续表

职业（工种）				企业人力资源管理师	等级		三级	
职业代码								
序号	鉴定点代码				鉴定内容	分数系数	重要系数	备注
	章	节	目	点				
108	4	2	1	3	关键事件法		5	
109	4	2	1	4	360 度评估方法		5	
	4	2	2		绩效评估过程组织		5	
110	4	2	2	1	绩效评估主体的选择		5	
111	4	2	2	2	绩效评估周期的确定		5	
112	4	2	2	3	绩效评估培训的实施		5	
113	4	2	2	4	绩效评估结果的评定		5	
	4	**3**			**绩效反馈与结果运用**		9	
	4	3	1		绩效反馈		9	
114	4	3	1	1	绩效反馈		5	
115	4	3	1	2	绩效面谈		9	
	4	3	2		绩效申诉机制		1	
116	4	3	2	1	绩效申诉的流程		1	
117	4	3	2	2	处理绩效评价投诉注意事项		1	
118	4	3	2	3	员工绩效评估结果申诉制度		1	
	4	3	3		绩效结果运用		5	
119	4	3	3	1	绩效评估结果应用的原则		1	
120	4	3	3	2	绩效评估结果应用需要防范的问题		5	
121	4	3	3	3	绩效评估结果应用的范围		5	
122	4	3	3	4	绩效改进的管理		5	
	5				**薪酬管理**	12		
	5	**1**			**岗位评价**			5
	5	1	1		岗位评价概述		5	
123	5	1	1	1	岗位评价的含义		1	
124	5	1	1	2	岗位评价的用途		5	
125	5	1	1	3	岗位评价的原则		5	
126	5	1	1	4	岗位评价的流程		9	

续表

职业（工种）				企业人力资源管理师	等级		三级	
序号	鉴定点代码				鉴定内容	分数系数	重要系数	备注
	章	节	目	点				
	5	1	2		岗位评价方法		5	
127	5	1	2	1	排序法		5	
128	5	1	2	2	分类套级法		5	
129	5	1	2	3	要素比较法		5	
130	5	1	2	4	要素计点法		5	
131	5	1	2	5	海氏评价法		5	
	5	**2**			**薪酬水平**		5	
	5	2	1		薪酬调查		5	
132	5	2	1	1	薪酬调查的目的		1	
133	5	2	1	2	薪酬调查的范围		1	
134	5	2	1	3	薪酬调查的渠道		5	
135	5	2	1	4	薪酬调查的程序		9	
	5	2	2		薪酬水平		5	
136	5	2	2	1	制约薪酬水平的因素		1	
137	5	2	2	2	薪酬水平策略的类型		5	
138	5	2	2	3	薪酬水平策略的选择		5	
139	5	2	2	4	薪酬水平调整的方法		5	
140	5	2	2	5	薪酬水平外部竞争力的体现		1	
	5	**3**			**薪酬结构设计**		5	
	5	3	1		薪酬结构设计概述		5	
141	5	3	1	1	薪酬结构设计的含义		1	
142	5	3	1	2	薪酬结构设计的目的		5	
143	5	3	1	3	薪酬结构设计的原则		5	
144	5	3	1	4	薪酬结构设计的流程		9	
	5	3	2		薪酬结构设计		5	
145	5	3	2	1	个体员工薪酬组成结构设计		5	
146	5	3	2	2	不同岗位员工之间的薪酬结构设计		5	

职业（工种）				企业人力资源管理师	等级		三级	
职业代码								

序号	鉴定点代码				鉴定内容	分数系数	重要系数	备注
	章	节	目	点				
	5	3	3		宽带薪酬		5	
147	5	3	3	1	宽带薪酬		5	
148	5	3	3	2	宽带薪酬的应用条件		5	
149	5	3	3	3	宽带薪酬的体系设计		5	
150	5	3	3	4	实施宽带薪酬应注意的问题		1	
	6				**劳动关系**	12		
	6	**1**			**员工关系管理**		5	
	6	1	1		员工关系管理概述		5	
151	6	1	1	1	员工关系与员工关系管理		5	
152	6	1	1	2	员工关系管理的必要性		5	
153	6	1	1	3	员工手册		5	
	6	1	2		劳动规章制度制定和实施		5	
154	6	1	2	1	劳动规章制度的含义		1	
155	6	1	2	2	劳动规章制度的内容		5	
156	6	1	2	3	劳动规章制度的制定程序		5	
157	6	1	2	4	劳动规章制度的法律效力		5	
	6	1	3		劳动纪律制定和实施		5	
158	6	1	3	1	劳动纪律		1	
159	6	1	3	2	劳动纪律的实施		5	
160	6	1	3	3	惩戒权的限制		1	
	6	**2**			**集体协商与集体合同**		9	
	6	2	1		集体协商		9	
161	6	2	1	1	集体协商的主体		5	
162	6	2	1	2	集体合同协商的过程		9	
163	6	2	1	3	集体协商注意的环节		5	
164	6	2	1	4	集体协商的技巧		5	
	6	2	2		集体合同管理		5	

续表

职业（工种）				企业人力资源管理师	等级		三级	
职业代码								
序号	章	节	目	点 鉴定内容	分数系数	重要系数	备注
165	6	2	2	1 集体合同的含义		1	
166	6	2	2	2 集体合同的特征		1	
167	6	2	2	3 集体合同的内容		5	
168	6	2	2	4 集体合同订立的原则		5	
169	6	2	2	5 集体合同的管理		5	
170	6	2	2	6 集体合同争议处理		9	
	6	3		**职工民主管理**		5	
	6	3	1	职工民主管理概述		5	
171	6	3	1	1 职工民主管理的概念		1	
172	6	3	1	2 职工民主管理的立法		5	
173	6	3	1	3 职工民主管理的形式		5	
	6	3	2	职工代表大会		9	
174	6	3	2	1 职工代表大会的性质		1	
175	6	3	2	2 职工代表大会的职权		5	
176	6	3	2	3 职工代表的权利和义务		9	
177	6	3	2	4 职工代表大会的主要程序		5	
	6	3	3	工会		5	
178	6	3	3	1 工会概述		1	
179	6	3	3	2 工会组织		1	
180	6	3	3	3 工会的权利和义务		5	

注：重要系数：以1、5、9表示，数字越大，重要程度越高。

附录2 《企业人力资源管理师》(三级) 操作技能鉴定要素细目表

职业（工种）			企业人力资源管理师	等级		三级	
职业代码							

序号	鉴定点代码			鉴定内容	分数系数	重要系数	备注
	项目	单元	点				
1	1			人力资源规划			
2	1	1		人力资源信息分析		5	
3	1	2		人力资源需求与供给预测		5	
4	1	3		人力资源动态平衡		9	
5	1	4		人力资源管理制度建设		5	
6	1	5		工作分析流程管理		9	
7	1	6		工作说明书编制		9	
8	2			招聘与配置			
9	2	1		编制招聘计划		9	
10	2	2		招聘广告分析与设计		9	
11	2	3		知识测验组织		5	
12	2	4		心理测验应用		5	
13	2	5		面试过程管理		9	
14	2	6		录用决策管理		5	
15	2	7		新员工入职管理		9	

续表

职业（工种）			企业人力资源管理师		等级	三级	
职业代码							
序号	鉴定点代码			鉴定内容	分数系数	重要系数	备注
	项目	单元	点				
16	2	8		离职面谈		5	
17	3			培训与开发			
18	3	1		搜集、整理、分析培训需求信息		9	
19	3	2		撰写培训需求分析报告		5	
20	3	3		培训目标的设定		5	
21	3	4		培训计划的编制		9	
22	3	5		培训组织的管理		9	
23	3	6		培训预算编制		5	
24	4			绩效管理			
25	4	1		制订绩效计划		5	
26	4	2		绩效目标的分解		5	
27	4	3		设计绩效评估表格		9	
28	4	4		绩效评估的实施		9	
29	4	5		绩效申诉管理		5	
30	4	6		绩效面谈		9	
31	5			薪酬福利管理			
32	5	1		岗位评价的流程		9	
33	5	2		市场薪酬调查		9	
34	5	3		薪酬满意度调查		5	
35	5	4		薪酬水平策略选择		5	
36	5	5		薪酬结构设计		5	
37	6			劳动关系管理			
38	6	1		员工手册编制		9	
39	6	2		劳动规章制度的编制		9	
40	6	3		劳动纪律的管理		5	
41	6	4		集体协商		5	
42	6	5		集体合同编制		5	
43	6	6		职工民主管理		5	

注：重要系数：以1、5、9表示，数字越大，重要程度越高。

附录3 专业英语词汇表

序号	认知词汇	中译词意
1	Absence	缺席
2	Acceptability	可接受性
3	Achievement tests	成就测试
4	Action plan	行动计划
5	Adverse impact	负面影响
6	Allowance	津贴，补助
7	Announcement	公告
8	Applicant	求职者
9	Application	申请
10	Appraisal	评价，评估
11	Appoint	任命
12	Arbitrary	仲裁
13	Assessment center	评价中心
14	Authority	权威
15	Audiovisual instruction	视听教学
16	Audit approach	审计法
17	Balanced scorecard	综合评价卡，平衡计分卡
18	Behavior modeling	行为模拟

序号	认知词汇	中译词意
19	Behavior – based program	行为改变计划
20	Benchmarks	基准
21	Benefits	福利
22	Bonus	奖金
23	Business planning	企业规划
24	Candidate	候选人
25	Career anchor	职业锚
26	Career counseling	职业咨询
27	Career curves	职业曲线
28	Career development	职业发展
29	Centralization	集权化
30	Coach	教练
31	Cognitive ability	认知能力
32	Commitment	承诺，义务
33	Communication skill	沟通技巧
34	Compensable factors	报酬要素
35	Compensation	报酬，补偿
36	Competency assessment	能力评估
37	Competency model	能力模型
38	Competitive advantage	竞争优势
39	Compromise	妥协
40	Concentration strategy	集中战略
41	Consultation	商量，请教
42	Continuous learning	持续学习
43	Coordination training	合作培训
44	Core competencies	核心竞争力
45	Cost structure	成本结构
46	Critical incident method	关键事件法
47	Cross – cultural preparation	跨文化准备
48	Cross – training	交叉培训

序号	认知词汇	中译词意
49	Cultural environment	文化环境
50	Cultural shock	文化冲击
51	Customer appraisal	顾客评估
52	Data flow diagram	数据流程图
53	Decentralization	分散化
54	Decision making	决策
55	Deficiency	缺乏
56	Delayering	扁平化
57	Demand forecasting	需求预测
58	Depression	沮丧
59	Development planning system	开发规划系统
60	Differential piece rate	差额计件工资
61	Direct costs	直接成本
62	Discipline	纪律
63	Dismiss	解雇
64	Disparate treatment	差别性对待
65	Diversity training	多元化培训
66	Dividends	红利
67	Discrimination	歧视
68	Downsizing	精简
69	Downward move	降级
70	Efficiency wage theory	效率工资理论
71	Egalitarian	平等主义
72	Earnings	所得，收入
73	Efficiency	效率
74	Employee empowerment	员工授权
75	Employee leasing	员工租借
76	Employee survey research	雇员调查与研究
77	Entrepreneur	企业家
78	Equal employment opportunity（EEO）	公平就业机会

续表

序号	认知词汇	中译词意
79	Ethics	道德
80	Exit interview	离职面谈
81	Expatriate	外派雇员
82	Expert systems	专家系统
83	Explicit knowledge	显性知识
84	External growth strategy	外部成长战略
85	External labor market	外部劳动力市场
86	Face to face discussion	当面讨论
87	Factor comparison system	因素比较法
88	Feedback	反馈
89	Flat hourly rate	小时工资率
90	Flextime	灵活的时间
91	Flowchart	流程图
92	Formal education programs	正规教育计划
93	Frame of reference	参照系
94	Functional job analysis, FJA	职能工作分析
95	Gain sharing plans	收益分享计划
96	Globalization	全球化
97	Goals and timetables	目标和时间表
98	Group mentoring program	群体指导计划
99	Head hunter	猎头
100	Healthy and safety	健康安全
101	High – performance work systems	高绩效工作系统
102	Hourly work	计时工资制
103	Human capital	人力资本
104	Human resource information system	人力资源信息系统
105	Human resource management	人力资源管理
106	Human resources planning, HRP	人力资源计划
107	Income	收入，收益
108	Indirect costs	间接成本

续表

序号	认知词汇	中译词意
109	Inflation	通货膨胀
110	Input	投入
111	Insurance	保险
112	Intellectual asset	知识资产
113	Internal analysis	内部分析
114	Internal growth strategy	内部成长战略
115	Internal labor force	内部劳动力
116	Internet	互联网
117	Internship programs	实习计划
118	Interview	面试
119	Industrialization	产业化
120	IT（Information Technology）	信息技术
121	Invest	投资
122	Job analysis	工作分析
123	Job classification system	工作分类法
124	Job description	工作描述
125	Job design	工作设计
126	Job enlargement	工作扩大化
127	Job enrichment	工作丰富化
128	Job evaluation	工作评价
129	Job ranking system	工作重要性排序法
130	Job rotation	工作轮换
131	Job satisfaction	工作满意度
132	Job specification	工作规范
133	Job structure	工作结构
134	Labor relations process	劳动关系进程
135	Leaderless group discussion	无领导小组讨论法
136	Learning organization	学习型组织
137	Line manager	直线经理
138	Maintenance of membership	会员资格维持

续表

序号	认知词汇	中译词意
139	Management by objectives, MBO	目标管理
140	Management forecasts	管理预测
141	Management process	管理过程
142	Manager appraisal	经理评估
143	Managing diversity	管理多元化
144	Manpower	人力，劳动力
145	Markov analysis	马尔可夫分析法
146	Material incentive	物质奖励
147	Mediation	调解
148	Mentor	导师
149	Merit guideline	绩效指南
150	Minimum wage	最低工资
151	Morale	士气
152	Motivation to learn	学习的动机
153	Needs assessment	（培训）需要评价
154	Night shift	夜班
155	Nonprofit organization	非营利组织
156	Occupation	职业
157	On‐the‐job training, OJT	在职培训
158	Opportunity to perform	实践的机会
159	Organization desgin and development	组织设计与发展
160	Organizational analysis	组织分析
161	Organiztion chart	组织结构图
162	Organization code	组织代码
163	Orientation	入职培训
164	Outplacement counseling	重新谋职咨询
165	Outsourcing	外包
166	Overpay	超额工资
167	Panel interview	小组面试
168	Pay claim	加薪要求

续表

序号	认知词汇	中译词意
169	Pay grade	工资等级
170	Pay structure	工资结构
171	Pay – for – performance standard	按绩效的报酬标准
172	Pay – policy line	工资政策线
173	Payroll	职工薪水册
174	Pension	养老金，退休金
175	Peer appraisal	同事评估
176	Performance appraisal	绩效评价
177	Performance feedback	绩效反馈
178	Performance management	绩效管理
179	Performance planning and evaluation	绩效规划与评价系统
180	Post	岗位，职位
181	Priority	优先
182	Person characteristics	个人特征
183	Personnel selection	人员甄选
184	Piecework	计件工资
185	Position analysis questionnaire, PAQ	职位分析问卷调查
186	Power distance	权力差距
187	Predictive validation	预测效度
188	Profit sharing	利润分享
189	Promotion	晋升
190	Psychological contract	心理契约
191	Questionnaire	调查问卷
192	Rapport	和谐，亲善
193	Readability	易读性
194	Readiness for training	培训准备
195	Reasoning ability	推理能力
196	Reconciliation	和解
197	Recognition	认可，承认
198	Recruitment	招募

续表

序号	认知词汇	中译词意
199	Redundancy	冗余
200	Reengineering	流程再造
201	Reject	拒绝，否决
202	Reinstatement	复职
203	Relational database	关联数据库
204	Reliability	信度
205	Remuneration	报酬
206	Reputation	声誉，名声
207	Retention plan	（核心人员）保持计划
208	Repatriation	归国准备
209	Replacement charts	替换表
210	Return on investment（ROI）	投资回报
211	Role analysis technique	角色分析技术
212	Role play	角色扮演
213	Senior management	高级管理层
214	Sick leave	病假
215	Self – appraisal	自我评估
216	Subcontracting	转包合同
217	Substantive reason	客观存在因素
218	Successor	后任
219	Supply forecasting	供给预测
220	Talent	才能，才干
221	Situational interview	情景面试
222	Skill inventories	技能量表
223	Skill – based pay	技能工资
224	Specificity	明确性
225	Spot bonus	即时奖金
226	Staffing tables	人员配置表
227	Strategic choice	战略选择
228	Strategic congruence	战略一致性

续表

序号	认知词汇	中译词意
229	Strategic human resource management	战略性人力资源管理
230	Strategy implementation	战略执行
231	Subordinate	下属
232	Succession planning	可持续发展计划
233	Tacit knowledge	隐性知识
234	Task analysis	任务分析
235	Team building	团队建设
236	Termination	终止
237	Total quality management（TQM）	全面质量管理
238	Training administration	培训管理
239	Training outcomes	培训结果
240	Trend analysis	趋势分析
241	Turnover	离职，流动
242	Utility	效用
243	Validity	效度
244	Verbal comprehension	语言理解能力
245	Vesting	既得利益
246	Voicing	发言
247	Wage and salary survey	薪资调查
248	Web – based training	网上培训
249	Welfare system	福利体系
250	Work permit/ Work certificate	就业许可证